The GREAT GARDENS of EUROPE

The GREAT GARDENS of EUROPE

Consultant
Eliana Ferioli

Author
Maria Brambilla

Translators
Sandra Cattich and Lole Valente Cattich

NEW HOLLAND PUBLISHERS

This edition first published in 2005 by
New Holland Publishers (UK) Ltd
London • Cape • Town • Sydney • Auckland

www.newhollandpublishers.com

Garfield House, 86–88 Edgware Road, London W2 2EA, UK

ISBN: 1 84537 085 6

© De Agostini Editore, Novara 2005
www.deagostini.it
Corso della Vittoria 91, 28100 Novara

Reproduction by Officine Grafiche Novara 1901 S.p.A. - Novara 2005
Printing by Legatoria del Verbano

CONTENTS

INTRODUCTION

A place to uplift the emotions, revisit nature, tame the elements, explore the fantastic, enjoy freedom ... a place for private contemplation but also a social platform ... the garden is, perhaps more than any other form of human expression, a mirror that reflects the culture and customs of a period. The 'journey through a garden' that this book proposes is therefore a stimulating way to cast an eye over 500 years of European history.

From the seventeenth-century Levens Hall in the English countryside, where you can still find hornbeam and boxwood hedges trimmed into fantastic shapes, to the sumptuous Versailles, where statues and fountains proclaim the glory of the Sun King; from the renaissance Villa Lante in Bagnaia to the scenic garden of Giverny 'painted' by Claude Monet with iris-and-water-lily brushstrokes; from the magical refinements of Arabic culture at Alhambra in Granada, to a garden of the Great North, where roses flourish at Baroniet Rosendal ... these are only some of the great gardens of Europe that this book presents – with spectacular images, a text that closely examines their fascinating histories, and useful information for those who wish to visit them.

Of course, we could have included many more, the gardening heritage of Europe is so rich and precious. The criteria for our selection included the historical period, the relation of the garden to the surrounding landscape, the architectural and artistic styles found in these gardens; as well as their magical ability to touch our hearts through the human stories they reveal ...

ELIANA FERIOLI

AUSTRIA · GERMANY

The Neptune Fountain (Schönbrunn, Austria)

8

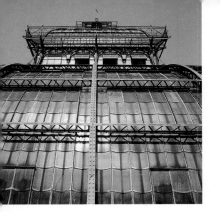

SCHÖNBRUNN *True symbol of 'Felix Austria',*
much-loved park of Maria Theresa and today a World Heritage Site.

The history of the imperial garden of Schönbrunn – declared by UNESCO a World Heritage Site for its perfectly preserved eighteenth-century layout – winds its way along a path of neglect and rediscovery, grandiose plans and sensible cut-backs, shameful destructions and proud reconstructions. It is a tortuous path begun in the Middle Ages, when the site of the present-day palace and park was called Katterburg – part of the monastery of Klosterneuburg, which boasted vines and orchards in a vast wood. In 1569 it was bought by the Habsburgs, who enclosed it and repopulated it with game of every type to satisfy their passion for hunting. It was on one of these hunting trips in 1612 that Emperor Matthias discovered the Fair Spring – Schöner Brunnen – that would change the name of the area forever from Katterburg to Schönbrunn.

Over the years, Schönbrunn transformed itself into a stylish country residence a few miles from the centre of Vienna. Equipped with an elegant Italian garden, parties, concerts and performances were organised out in the open for the pleasure of the Austrian sovereigns and their court. These carefree days were rudely interrupted, however, in 1683 when Schönbrunn was devastated by the Turks, who had beaten a path to the gates of Vienna, threatening the Habsburg Emperor and the whole of Europe. This was an insult to avenge at any cost, and so, a few years later, to celebrate the end of the long Ottoman siege, Leopold I ordered the construction of a luxurious palace directly on the ruins of the old hunting lodge. In

consultation was Johann Bernhard Fisher von Erlach, architect of the court, who imagined a stately palace triumphantly raised on the crest of a hill, ideally from where the Austrian home would dominate the city and the plain as far as the eye could see. It was an alluring plan, but unfortunately too costly for the actual budget. Fisher von Erlach therefore developed a simpler version that envisaged a more modest building on the plain, enriched by an immense green space and inspired by the principles that the great André Le Nôtre had employed at the royal palace park at Versailles: in front of the palace façade, a vast *parterre de broderie* was composed of flowerbeds, swirls of boxwood and coloured gravel; this was arranged symmetrically along the principal axis, and was flanked on both sides by wide boskets, furrowed by straight avenues that directed the eye towards the surrounding countryside and created an impression of infinite space.

The construction of the hunting lodge and park began in 1696 and continued for years, interrupted repeatedly by a chronic shortage of funds. Basins were dug, fountains were built, 20,000 beech trees were bought to thicken the boskets, Dutch flowers were imported to decorate the Great Parterre, yews arrived from France, and boxwood from Italy. But in 1728, the already slow construction works stopped completely: Charles VI, emperor of the period, rarely went to Schönbrunn, and then only to shoot the pheasants bred in the game preserve, so a period of neglect began for the

LEFT AND ABOVE: *STAR FOUNTAIN AND ACCOMPANYING ROUND FOUNTAIN. CREATED BETWEEN 1770 AND 1780 IN VIPITENO MARBLE, THESE ARE SITUATED IN FRONT OF THE PALACE, ON THE EAST AND WEST SIDES OF THE GREAT PATERRE, AT POINTS ON THE STAR-SHAPED SYSTEM OF AVENUES. BOTH REPRESENT THE NAIADS, OR WATER NYMPHS.*
OPPOSITE: *THE PORTRAIT OF MARIA THERESA, EMPRESS OF AUSTRIA BY MARTIN VAN MEYTENS (1695-1770)* OPPOSITE, TOP: *DETAIL OF THE GREAT PALM HOUSE.*

TOP: THE GREAT PALM HOUSE, BUILT BETWEEN 1881 AND 1882 IN STEEL AND GLASS. IT IS 113 METRES LONG, MADE UP OF A CENTRAL PAVILLION 28 METRES HIGH, AND TWO SIDE PAVILLIONS 25 METRES HIGH. A STEAM HEATING SYSTEM RECREATES THE APPROPRIATE CLIMATE FOR PLANTS FROM ALL OVER THE WORLD. ABOVE, LEFT: A CORNER OF THE PARK WITH SEVERAL PLANTS TRIMMED INTO SHAPE. ABOVE, RIGHT: ONE OF THE STAR PATHS, DEFINED BY TREES TRAINED INTO ESPALIER.

OPPOSITE, TOP: THE 'GLORIETTE', BUILT IN 1775 ON THE CREST OF THE HILL THAT RISES AT THE END OF THE GREAT PARTERRE. ITS ARCHED BUILDING AND FLAT ROOF SERVE AS A PANORAMIC VIEWING TERRACE. AT THE FOOT OF THE HILL IS THE NEPTUNE FOUNTAIN, WHICH REPRESENTS THE SEA GOD ON HIS SHELL-SHAPED CHARIOT. OPPOSITE, BELOW: THE CENTRAL PAVILLION OF THE OLD SERAGLIO, TODAY ENLARGED AND TRANSFORMED INTO A ZOOLOGICAL GARDEN.

hunting lodge and gardens. Twelve years later this was interrupted by the enthronement of Maria Theresa, the empress who, unlike Charles VI, adored Schönbrunn to the point that she made it the centre of her court and of political life. As a result of her efforts, an intensive programme of works got underway to reconstruct the old hunting lodge. Enlarged and adorned with valuable fittings, it became a sumptuous imperial palace in the rococo style. Work on the garden also got underway: without changing Fisher von Erlach's ground plans, the design now included a new green space, more in keeping with the times and more aligned to the new sovereign's taste – a space that has remained substantially unchanged to this day.

SERAGLIO: THE LURE OF THE EXOTIC

The seraglio of Schönbrunn is one of many places that demonstrate how common rare birds and animals were in the parks of princes and sovereigns. Their exotic appeal would impress guests and in this way enhance the sovereign's power. In 1819, Ferdinand I de Bourbon wasted no time in sending 18 papyrus scrolls that had emerged from the ashes of Herculaneum to England in exchange for kangaroos to put in his Floridiana Park in Naples – a rash compromise to satisfy a passion that he shared with the ancient Assyrian kings, who surrounded their palaces with game preserves that included animals from distant countries: lions, ostriches and monkeys. Collections of exotic animals also decorated the fabulous Persian gardens described by Senofonte, which captured the imagination of the Greeks and the Romans. To emulate these eastern paradises, in the park surrounding Varrone's villa in Tuscolo, wild boar and deer roamed freely and wild goats came running at the sound of a horn. And at the beginning of the sixteenth century, Pope Leo X installed a real zoo in his Vatican residence, with parrots, monkeys, elephants, lions, civets and chameleons. Yet the most spectacular seraglio (now no longer) was undoubtedly that created for the Sun King at Versailles – the habitual destination of the daily walks of the sovereign and his courtiers. This was an elegant construction, probably designed by Louis le Vau, with a large, octagonal, dome-shaped hall surrounded by courtyards that radiated from the centre, supplied with little canals, ponds and jets of water for the exotic animals – African birds, small mammals, as well as an elephant and a rhinoceros.

First came the remodelling of the Great Parterre in front of the palace façade: eight flowerbeds, symmetrically arranged in pairs along the central axis of the garden to form an English parterre, lawns decorated by platbands (borders of flowers) and subtle spirals of flowering plants. In the vast ornamental boskets on either side of the Great Parterre, the gardeners of the Empress, under the direction of the architect Johann Ferdinand Hetzendorf von Hohenberg, traced a new system of star-shaped avenues, which, instead of directing the gaze towards a distant horizon, as they did in the plans of Fisher von Erlach, arrested the gaze on a group of statues, fountains and pavilions. At the end of a very long, left diagonal axis, the Obelisk Fountain – in baroque iconography, the symbol of sovereign stability – took shape, while the right diagonal axis ended with a seraglio that brings to mind, on a smaller scale, that of the Sun King at Versailles: thirteen animal cages arranged in lines that radiated from an elegant central pavilion fitted with wooden panels, mirrors, and paintings of

TOP: *THE ROMAN RUIN, CREATED IN 1778 AS ROMANTIC SCENERY. THE USE OF MOCK RUINS IN GARDENS HAD BEGUN IN ENGLAND IN THE EIGHTEENTH CENTURY. THE RUIN REPRESENTS AN ANCIENT ROMAN TEMPLE, WITH COLUMNS, ORNAMENTS AND BUSTS. ABOVE: IN THE POND, TWO STATUES DEDICATED TO THE GODS OF THE DANUBE AND ENNS RIVERS. OPPOSITE, TOP: THE BOSKET WITH THE STATUES OF OLYMPIA AND ALEXANDER, IN THE BACKGROUND THE PALACE.; BELOW: ONE OF THE PARK'S STATUES.*

rare animals and birds. Francis I de Lorraine, husband of the Empress and a great enthusiast of the natural sciences, visited each day to admire the animals and to take his breakfast. At the end of the nineteenth century, this precious seraglio, the only one to survive among those that decorated the great parks of the past, was enlarged and new enclosures formed to house a modern zoological garden.

Maria Theresa also arranged for the hill at the end of the Great Parterre to finish the perspective of the long central axis. At the foot of the hill, the Neptune Fountain was built, flanked by two flights of stairs and circled by trees. On the crest of the hill, exactly where Fisher von Erlach originally wanted the palace to stand, she created the 'Gloriette', with its arches, flat roof and balustrade providing a perfect belvedere. For the slope of the hill, Hetzendorf von Hohenberg had ambitious plans, imagining the descent of a bounding cascade, flanked by ornamental columns, equestrian statues and triumphant arches. Maria Theresa declined these in favour of

were open to the public from the end of the nineteenth century.) Recently, the labyrinth was restored, following the old layout as much as possible and including the raised platform at the end of the path.

The botanical garden, the area where Maria Theresa's husband personally acclimatised the rare plants sent to him from all over the world, has disappeared entirely. In its place, between 1881 and 1882, appeared the Great Palm House, an exceptionally large building made of steel and glass, where the concave and convex lines of its powerful ribbings alternate harmoniously. More than 100 metres long, it includes a 28-metre high central pavilion and two side pavilions that are 2 metres lower. Here, thanks to a steam-powered heating system that was avant-garde in its time, plants from all the continents still thrive today.

something infinitely more sober – a verdant expanse of lawn with two zig-zag paths: a form closer to the serpentine lines that were just beginning to appear in English landscaped parks.

On either side of the Great Parterre are wide boskets that are traversed by long avenues and bordered by thick hedges pruned according to the art of topiary, where the branches of the trees sometimes fold over to form endlessly green tunnels. Amongst these avenues some of the most elegant enclosures were created. These were designed in every shape and size imaginable: squares, trapezoids, ovals, circles – all protected by high walls of trees planted in orderly rows and trained into espaliers. These secluded, out-of-the-way spots contained open-air rooms with pavilions, water basins, statues dedicated to mythological figures, and, as a tribute to the new taste for romantic scenes, even a mock Roman ruin.

Among the trees of the boskets, Maria Theresa's gardeners laid down a labyrinth, a path that wound its way between two imposing walls of yews until one reached a central point occupied by an elevated pavilion, which allowed one to view the entire path. Continuously neglected in the course of the nineteenth century, the labyrinth was removed in 1892 because 'it lent itself to illicit meetings in public places'. (The Schönbrunn gardens

WHERE: The park and the Grand Palace of Schönbrunn (declared a World Heritage Site by UNESCO) are on the Schönbrunner Schlossstraße in Vienna.

GETTING THERE: By underground (U4), tram (no. 10 or 58) or bus (10 A). In all three cases, get off at the stop for Schönbrunn.

VISITING HOURS: The gardens are open all day from daybreak to dusk. Guided tours are available.

INFORMATION: tel.0043 1 8775087; fax. 0043 1 8775067; e-mail: webmaster@schoenbrunn.at; or visit www.schoenbrunn.at

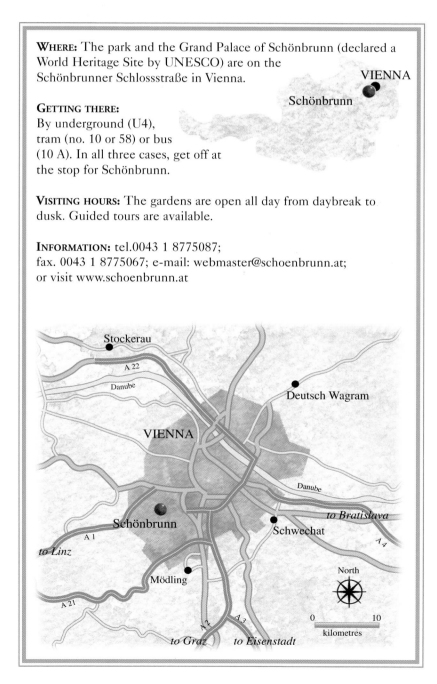

HELLBRUNN *An enchanted palace whose astonishing trick fountains hold as much delight today as they did four centuries ago.*

In seventeenth-century Europe, gardens were already established as a means of exhibiting the wealth and influence of princes and sovereigns, indispensable frameworks for phantasmagoric shows, parties and open-air lunches organised to arouse the admiration of friends and the envy of enemies. For precisely this reason, in 1612, Markus Sittikus of Hohenems, recently elected archbishop of Salzburg, wasted no time in entrusting the Italian architect Santino Solari with the task of building a country residence surrounded by a green space that would hold up well against the fantastic Italianate gardens then in fashion. The spot chosen for the new residence was at the foot of the Hellbrunn hill, at the gates of Salzburg: a pleasing area rich in the water sources necessary to realise a garden to parallel those that embellished the refined De' Medici towns in Tuscany, or the sumptuous summer residences of the Roman cardinals in the Latium countryside. These were spaces designed with a set-square and plumb-line and decorated with plants arranged in geometrical forms and, notably, with trick fountains capable of evoking astonishment and admiration in visitors. These water features included spectacular fountains, sprays of water that suddenly surprised guests, and water automatons that exploited the sophisticated mechanisms invented by Hero, a mathematician born in Alexandria in the first century AD and rediscovered by Italian Renaissance engineers. These were decidedly fascinating devices, that had transformed many gardens of the time into places devoted to amusement and intrigue, entertaining visitors and provoking astonishment and curiosity by means of the complex technology employed.

Not to disappoint the expectations of his venerable client, Santino Solari drew inspiration from the most admired of these gardens – that which surrounded the villa created by Bernardo Buontalenti for Francesco I de' Medici in Pratolino, not far from Florence. The many marvels conceived in this garden were punctually reproduced in the garden of Hellbrunn, earning the latter the the name of 'Pratolino of the North'. Just as spectators did in the villa of Francesco I, one could, and still can, admire the small mechanical theatres representing scenes from daily life, everything from a mill to a grinder's shop. Also identical to those in Pratolino were the decorations of sponges and shells that lined the walls of several artificial caves – mysterious grottoes where light alternated with shade, and fear with delight. In the most spectacular, dedicated to Neptune, a hydraulically operated figure rolls his eyes and sticks his tongue out, while small mechanical birds perched on the walls sing out for all to hear. There is also a grotto filled with mirrors, and another inhabited by a dragon that springs out of his den to drink at a fountain. At Hellbrunn, water is the central theme of the garden: in the form of canals, wide parterres and streams that flank the paths. Even on the exterior walls of the palace, water animates fountains in the form of deer heads or hunting trophies. It gushes out from unexpected points to drench visitors and pours over unfortunate guests as they sit down to relax. There is even a marble table with a central basin to chill wine and preserve food on sultry summer days. These sophistications were also found in other Renaissance gardens, for example at the Villa Lante in Bagnaia, invented many centuries before by Plinio for his own villa in Tuscany.

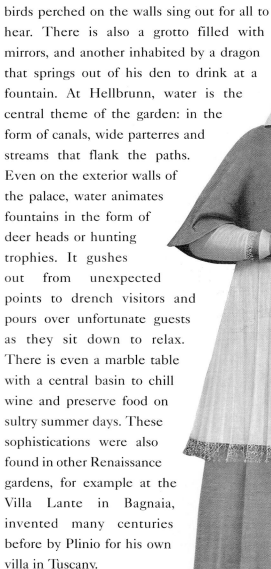

ABOVE: *VIEW OF THE CASTLE AND GARDEN OF HELLBRUNN. THE VAST FRENCH-STYLE PARTERRE, WITH FLOWERBEDS THAT LOOK LIKE EMBROIDERED MATS, WAS ADDED IN THE EIGHTEENTH CENTURY, WHILE THE OVERALL LAYOUT OF THE ESTATE GOES BACK TO THE PREVIOUS CENTURY. IN FACT, IT WAS IN 1612 THAT MARKUS SITTIKUS OF HOHENEMS, ARCHBISHOP OF SALZBURG (OPPOSITE), COMMISSIONED THE ITALIAN ARCHITECT, SANTINO SOLARI, TO BUILD THIS COUNTRY RESIDENCE. RIGHT: THE CASTLE FAÇADE. OPPOSITE, TOP: DETAIL OF A UNICORN STATUE.*

WHEN ITALIAN STYLE LED THE WAY

Markus Sittikus's decision to entrust an Italian architect with the design of his country palace at Hellbrunn confirmed the fact that, until the appearance of the park at Versailles designed by Le Nôtre, the Renaissance gardens of Tuscany and Latium set the trend for all of Europe. This was an unquestioned supremacy, supported by the enthusiastic reports of English, French and German travellers, who had visited Pratolino or the garden of Villa d'Este at Tivoli. It was therefore inevitable that princes and sovereigns would seek the collaboration of Italian artists in order to implement the desired gardening innovations in their own homes. For the De' Medicis, the Dukes of Tuscany and all proprietors of enviable green spaces, the dispatch of hydraulic engineers and gardeners to foreign countries had become a means to obtain favours and strengthen political alliances. In the second half of the sixteenth century, for example, Francesco I sent to Emperor Maximilian of Austria, from whom he hoped to obtain the title of archduke, the plans of his palace garden and two gardeners. While at the end of the sixteenth century, Ferdinando I reinforced his friendship with the French king, Henry IV, by sending the Francini brothers, valued creators of the Pratolino automatons, to his court. On a more modest level, the gift for William of Vittelsbach consisted only of the shells necessary to decorate a grotto in his Bavarian Monaco residence.

SOME OF THE TRICK FOUNTAINS FOR WHICH THE HELLBRUNN PALACE IS SO RIGHTLY FAMOUS. ABOVE: CROWN GROTTO. LEFT: FOUNTAIN IN THE FORM OF A DEER'S HEAD WITH JETS OF WATER ISSUING FROM ITS MOUTH. OPPOSITE, TOP: THE MARBLE TABLE AROUND WHICH MARKUS SITTIKUS SEATED HIS GUESTS. THE LONG, NARROW BASIN IN THE CENTRE KEPT WINE AND FOOD FRESH ON SULTRY SUMMER DAYS, BUT UNFORTUNATE GUESTS WERE ALSO 'REFRESHED' BY SUDDEN JETS OF WATER AS SOON AS THEY SAT ON THE BENCHES. THE TRICK FOUNTAINS STILL FUNCTION TODAY.

WHERE: The palace and gardens of Hellbrunn lie on the southern periphery of Salzburg.

GETTING THERE: By car, take the A10 and exit at the southern side of Salzburg; by bus, take the 55 towards St. Leonhard from the central station in Salzburg.

VISITING HOURS: Between April and October, guided tours of the palace and fountains are available from 9:00 to 16:30. This is extended to 17:30 between May and September and, in July and August, evening tours of the trick fountains are available until 22:00.

INFORMATION: tel. 0043 6628203720; fax. 0043 6628203724931; e-mail: schloss.hellbrunn@stadt-salzburg.at; or visit www.hellbrunn.at

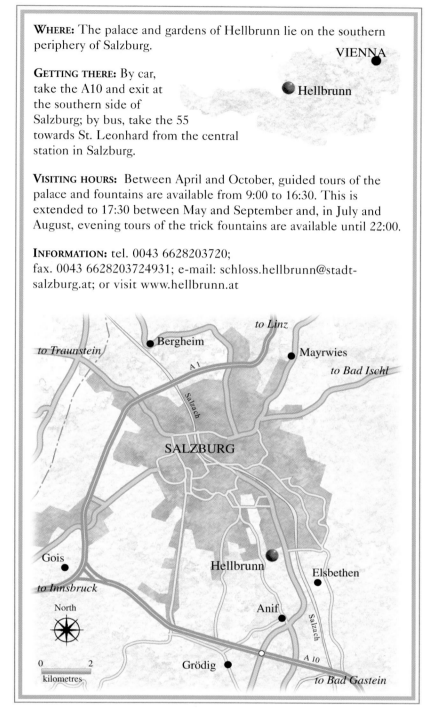

In the eighteenth century, the Renaissance layout of Hellbrunn was partly modified by the introduction of a vast French-style parterre, and the list of marvels lengthened with the delightful mechanical theatre created by Lorenz Rosenegger: a miniature masterpiece reproducing a market square and craft shops and animated by 200 water-propelled marionettes. Some time later, the green space extending from the southern side of the palace was divided into an extensive English-style park, as the fashion of the day dictated. This transformation did not diminish the true glory of Hellbrunn – the subtle trick fountains and the still perfectly functional water automatons – and, unlike Pratolino and practically all other Renaissance gardens, it survives still.

19

VEITSHÖCHHEIM *The summer residence of the prince-bishops of Würzburg, and the most fascinating rococo garden in Europe.*

In a little more than ten years, between 1763 and 1776, the green space around the summer residence of the prince-bishops of Würzburg had discarded an unsuccessful baroque design to become the most appealing rococo garden in Europe. This was an eccentric and sophisticated garden, impossible to capture at a single glance because the grandiose, strict French layout that had governed Europe for almost a century had been broken up into intimate and agreeable little pieces; a splendid frame for the entertainment of a bright, cultured aristocracy.

Veitshöchheim started to take form in 1680, when Peter Philipp von Dernbach ordered the construction of a hunting lodge (soon to become a more comfortable summer residence) a few miles from his royal palace in Würzburg. Given the nature of the existing grounds, the garden had to be laid out along two central and parallel axes and divided into two separate parts: the parterre, which consisted of four flowerbeds around the castle, and a lower section consisting of three long, narrow strips of ground. It was a design that went entirely against the rule and style of the period – a single central axis that would link the castle, parterre, garden and wood in a strict logical and spatial sequence.

In 1763, another prince-bishop, Adam Friedrich von Seinsheim, decided to embellish the garden without upsetting the old layout. In this way, the two sections of the garden that had been maintained independently for almost eighty years, preserved their autonomy, linked

RIGHT: THE PALACE LIES AT THE CENTRE OF A RAISED TERRACE ABOVE THE GARDEN, ACCESSED BY MEANS OF TWO FLIGHTS OF STAIRS. OPPOSITE: THE FOCAL POINT OF THE GARDEN: THE GREAT LAKE WITH ITS SCULPTURAL WORKS BY FERDINAND TIETZ. THIS REPRESENTS MOUNT PARNASSUS, APOLLO AND THE NINE MUSES, AND PEGASUS, WHO TOWERS ABOVE, SPREADING HIS WINGS TOWARDS OLYMPUS. TOP: WINGED GUESTS ON THE BANKS OF THE GREAT LAKE.

only by the use of telescopes, garden paths and flights of stairs. In the area around the castle, in the place of four rather old-fashioned flowerbeds, we now find a *parterre de broderie* with elegant forms of boxwood. Among the three strips of lower ground, strictly separated by paths bordered by linden and fir trees, we find unusual pavilions, secluded green rooms enclosed by hornbeam hedgerows and an infinite number of sculptures that the Master of the House commissioned from Ferdinand Tietz. These included shepherds that played and danced, puttos, artistic allegories from the five continents and allegories expressing the four seasons – figures that expressed the joie de vivre typical of the

period and that helped to create that particularly fresh garden atmosphere: light, bright, and far from daily preoccupations.

On the first strip of ground, in the centre of an immense stretch of water, rise the crags of Parnassus, where Pegasus is about to launch into a conquest of the heavens. The second strip immediately next to it accommodates a circular lawn enclosed by hedges, connected via winding avenues bordered by hornbeams to a maze of green rooms and trellised pavilions. In the third area, populated with densely crowded trees, we find fountains, a grotto with a belvedere and a hedged theatre, the stage crowded with characters from the *commedia del arte*.

Stretches of water, avenues of linden and fir trees, a wood, fountains, green rooms enclosed by walls of hornbeam and statues: the garden of Veitshöchheim is an ensemble of different elements, typical of the variety we associate with the rococo style. The trellised pavilion (opposite, top right) is one of the more famous structures.

23

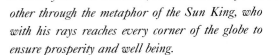

STONE HEROES

In the great gardens of the past, statues were indispensable embellishments, an effective means to signal the cultural standing of the owner, to show off the wealth of the family, and to extol their distinguished, if improbable, origins. In the sixteenth century, for example, the powerful Roman cardinals filled the parks of their villas with the busts of ancient emperors, heroes and mythological figures. Brought to light by archaeological excavations, they were exhibited in the most visible parts of the garden – areas chosen precisely to show off these valuable, antiquarian collections. If they weren't able to procure ancient statues, then new ones worked very well. These had the advantage of encouraging the invention of grandiose allegorical tales, translated into artistic forms by the more valued artists of the period. Cosimo I de' Medici populated the garden of his castle at the gates of Florence with figures sculpted by Ammannati and Giambologna. These illustrated the qualities of the Grand Duke's family: a statue of Hercules and Antaeus to proclaim the victory of virtue, another of Venus to announce the beginning of the golden age that Cosimo had promised. A century later at Versailles, at the residence of Louis XIV, the story of Apollo unfolds from one corner of the immense park to the other through the metaphor of the Sun King, who with his rays reaches every corner of the globe to ensure prosperity and well being.

Light, merry, ironic: around 300 statues, almost all created by the sculptor Ferdinand Tietz, decorate the garden of Veitshöchheim. Opposite: the belvedere and the amazing grotto. The niches in the rocaille walls reveal wolves, foxes, owls, dragons and other fantastic animals made from stones and shells.

WHERE: Veitshöchheim is 17 kilometres north of Würzburg, Hofgarten 1.

GETTING THERE: By car from Würzburg along freeway no. 3 or 7, take the Würzburg Centre exit and follow the directions for the castle; by bus from Würzburg, take no. 11 or 19 leaving from Kirchplatz.

VISITING HOURS: Every day, except 24, 25, 31 December and 1 January, from 9:00 to 18:00 in the summer and from 9:00 to 17:30 in the winter.

INFORMATION: tel. 0049 931 355170; e-mail: sgvwuerzburg@ bsv.bayern.de; or visit www.schloesser.bayern.de

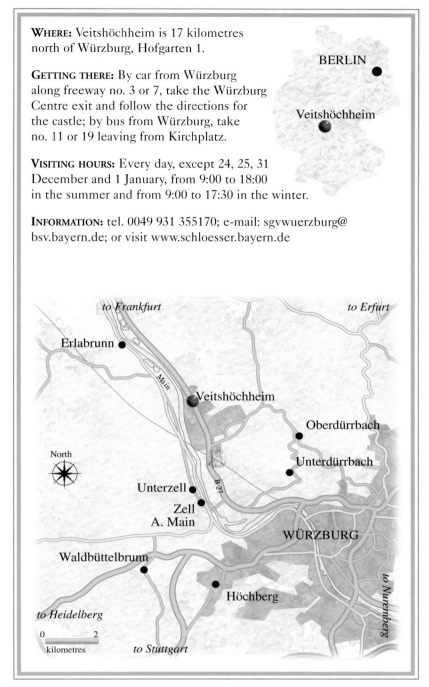

Today, many statues have been replaced with reproductions. In a corner of the woods, where a Chinese Pavilion was created for enjoyable lunches in the open, with sandstone benches and mock palms in green and red stone acting as supports for the blue cupola decorated by a gold pineapple, the garish colours that once made the pavilion so striking have disappeared. Despite the inevitable decline caused by passing time, Veitshöchheim nonetheless managed to escape the capricious evolution of garden styles. This was due to the interest shown by the King of Bavaria, Maximilian Joseph, in the first years of the nineteenth century who, as a true romantic, fell in love with the old rococo garden and prevented its transformation into a landscape garden.

ISLE OF MAINAU *The 'Flower Island' sits above the Lake of Constance and is always in bloom.*

A Renaissance cross greets visitors at the beginning of the footbridge that joins the coast of the Lake of Constance to Mainau. This Swedish Cross, nailed into the floor, witnessed the dramatic raid of the island by the Swedish Army in 1647 – and was one of the few precious objects that was not looted by soldiers. Between 1272 and 1806 the island was governed by the religious Teutonic Order. The island had many owners – among these, Friedrich I, Grand Duke of Baden, Mainau – and geographically it belonged to Baden-Württemberg. But from 1907 it became the property of the Swedish royal family, who inherited it via relations of Friedrich I. The botanical wealth that has earned Mainau the name 'Flower Island' is due to the current owner, Prince Lennart Bernadotte, who has personally seen to the restoration of both the castle, designed in 1773 by the architect Johann Caspar Bagnato, and the gardens. After studying Agricultural and Forest Sciences, the Prince has worked closely with the Deutsche Garten-Gesellschaft, the German Gardening Foundation, which from 1882 has preserved and promoted gardening cultures.

To the eyes of visitors today, Mainau appears as a gigantic

RIGHT: *THE ITALIAN STAIRCASE, A SPECTACULAR WATERFALL LINKING THE HIGHER PORTION OF THE CASTLE WITH THE LAKESIDE, IS FLANKED BY A PROFUSION OF FLOWERS THAT CHANGE WITH THE SEASONS: TULIPS, VIOLETS, NARCISSUSES IN SPRING; OLEANDERS, GAZANIAS, MALLOWS, HELIO-TROPES AND ROSES IN SUMMER.*

ABOVE: *A CORNER OF THE ITALIAN ROSE GARDEN. OPPOSITE: A GLIMPSE OF THE GARDEN CLOSE TO THE CASTLE AND THE BAROQUE CHURCH ST MARIA; TOP: ONE OF THE 40,000 ROSES ON THE ISLAND.*

collection of gardens and flowering zones that are active in every season. Its 45 hectares of ground contain everything the enthusiast could hope for. Along the south side of the castle, for example, rose lovers cannot miss the Italian Rose Garden, framed by an old pergola created by Friedrich I in 1871. The Rose Garden hosts as many as 9,000 roses belonging to 400 different varieties, although you will find at least 30,000 examples of around 1,200 species and cultivars bedded out in other parts of the island – along the Road of Roses, for example, which hosts a collection internationally renowned for its historical value, or in the Information Garden, created to provide news of developments for all lovers of these flowers.

Those with a weakness for spring flowers need to visit Mainau between April and May and walk along the avenues of chestnut and plane trees, which wind their way through the southern parts of the island among meadows sprinkled with flowering cherry trees, at the foot of which blooms a sea of tulips, narcissuses, hyacinths, crocuses, etc. – something like 1,200,000 bulbs, surrounded by 200,000 violets and primroses. To the west of the castle, near a medieval donjon that

ABOVE AND TOP: *THE PEACOCK, THE DUCKLING AND MANY OTHER ANIMALS MADE OF FLOWERS IN THE* KINDERLAND, *A PLAY AREA RESERVED FOR CHILDREN. THEY ARE FORMED BY A STEEL FRAME FILLED WITH EARTH, DRESSED WITH A LAYER OF COMPOST AND HELD TOGETHER BY A WIRE NET THAT HOLDS THE FLOWERS.* OPPOSITE: *SPRING BLOOMS.*

LEFT AND BELOW: *THE ITALIAN ROSE GARDEN, FRAMED BY A PERGOLA ERECTED IN 1871 BY FRIEDRICH I OF BADEN. IT INCLUDES AROUND 9,000 ROSES BELONGING TO 400 DIFFERENT VARIETIES. OPPOSITE: THE MOBILE GREENHOUSE, USED TO COVER THE CASTLE TERRACE FOR SEVERAL MONTHS IN THE YEAR, SHELTERING PALMS, ORANGES, LEMONS AND EXOTIC BIRDS.*

WHERE: In the basin of Lake Constance, close to the headland of Bodanrücken, in Baden-Württemberg.

GETTING THERE: By boat from Constance or from Überlingen; by bus: no. 4 from Constance station; by car from Constance. Access to the island is via a footbridge.

VISITING HOURS: The gardens are open all year: between 26 March and 19 October, from 7:00 to 20:00; and between 20 October and 25 March, from 9:00 to 18:00.

INFORMATION: tel. 0049 75 31-303-0; fax. 0049 75 31-303-166; e-mail: souvenir@mainau.de; or visit www.mainau.de

dates back to a period of the Teutonic Order, vast meadows of flowers stretch out with tulips in spring and begonias, sage, *Impatiens* and *Ageratum* in summer. The whole area, named the 'Garden of Flowers', is dotted with solitary trees and thriving bushes of reeds (*Canna indica*).

The oldest garden occupies the terrace next to the castle: created by Friedrich I, it takes on the character of its Mediterranean plants: oranges, lemons, and a 14-metre palm (*Phoenix canariensis*). The terrace remains open to the elements until the middle of October, when it is covered by a large, mobile greenhouse, where orchid shows are organised in the winter months. Still next to the castle, we find the Tropical Garden, filled with bananas and other exotic plant species, like the Peruvian tomato tree (*Cyphomandra betacea*), the coffee plant (*Coffea arabica*), olives, eucalyptuses and a gigantic *Yucca elephantipes*.

Mainau is all this and more; other of its notable sights include the Garden of the Dahlias; the Garden of Azaleas and Rhododendrons; the pond in the Garden of Butterflies; the Garden of Aromatic and Medicinal Herbs; the Garden for Everyone; the Experience of Nature, which has real animals for children to pet; and *Kinderland*, which entertains children with its animals made of flowers. Lastly, there is the Italian Staircase, a cascade of water flanked by a profusion of flowers, linking the higher part of the island to the lake.

SANSSOUCI *With 290 hectares of parks and gardens, studded with palaces and lakes, Sanssouci is considered the 'Versailles of Germany'.*

For Frederick II of Hohenzollern (Frederick the Great), Sanssouci ('without worries') was supposed to be more than a leisurely royal palace; it was a refuge deep in nature where he could rest between wars, forgetting the intrigues and oppressive ceremonies of court. Between 1744 and 1764, under the supervision of the architect Georg Wenzeslaus won Knobelsdorff, and based on a sketch by Frederick II, plans for a summer house took form at Potsdam, Brandenberg. It was definitely refined, but modest in size: 97 metres long, 12 metres high, single-storied with only 12 rooms – not many for a royal residence.

Inaugurated with pomp and ceremony on 1 May in 1747 at a banquet for 200 invitees, the palace is situated on the summit of a hill. It is reached after a long walk across the park, from where it overlooks the terraced garden, which remains one of the attractions of Sanssouci since its restoration to its old splendour in the 1980s. Divided by a staircase of 132 steps, the six terraces were intended for fruit cultivation. Along the 3-metre walls that surround these terraces, there are 168 niches enclosed by mobile glass doors. Here the fig trees were sheltered in winter, comforted by the heat from charcoal burners when the temperatures dropped dangerously low. Cherry, apricot and peach trees were cultivated on special green trellises propped against the walls between the niches. Even today, yews trimmed into pyramidal forms, and citrus and pomegranate trees planted in vases, are arranged on the borders of each terrace to form a counterpoint to the niches and trellises.

At the foot of the terraces lay the *parterres de broderie*, and further out, the grassy parterres. The borders were filled with tulips, narcissuses, hyacinths, crocuses, primulas, auriculas and irises in spring, and with lilies, asters, mallows, jasmine and roses in summer. The centre was dominated by a large fountain with a basin in the form of an four-leafed clover, decorated by a group of gilded sculptures representing Teti. Rows of chestnut and walnut trees framed the garden on its sides. Today the parterres no longer exist and the basin has been modified, but the composition nonetheless preserves the harmony and formal equilibrium of the original.

Within little more than a century, numerous buildings and a vast park sprung up around the palace and its orchard-garden, until Sanssouci was transformed into the enormous complex now considered the 'Versailles of Germany'. As such it was appropriately declared a World Site Heritage in 1991.

To celebrate the victory of the Seven Year War (1756–1763) Frederick II ordered the construction of the New Palace, a rococo building so sumptuous and so impressive (213 metres long, with 322 windows, 230 columns and 428 statues) that the Sovereign himself described it as a real 'fanfaronade'. The palace looks out onto a long avenue that constitutes the central axis of the park, designed by the botanist and architect Peter Joseph Lenné, and commissioned at the beginning of the nineteenth century after a complete restructuring of the gardens.

Crossing the vast park, which is scored with a network of avenues and lanes, one can admire a series of somewhat surprising architectural styles. For example, the Chinese Tea House, which is decorated with gilded stucco, statues and a roof in the form of an awning, which is crowned by a Mandarin holding a glittering, golden umbrella; or the Roman Baths, a complex of buildings modelled on ancient Roman homes and on Herculaneum, which have always been used as the

LEFT: *THE PALACE OF SANSSOUCI WITH ITS ORCHARD-GARDEN, FORMED OVER SIX TERRACES DIVIDED BY A STATELY STAIRCASE. TODAY, FRUIT TREES AND VINES ARE CULTIVATED ON THE TERRACES, JUST AS IN THE TIMES OF FREDERICK II OF PRUSSIA (IN THE PORTRAIT OPPOSITE).*
ABOVE: *ONE OF THE HORNBEAM PERGOLAS THAT SHADE THE PATHS IN FRONT OF THE ORANGERY. OPPOSITE, TOP: DETAIL OF ONE OF THE TWO WROUGHT IRON PAVILIONS ON THE SIDES OF THE PALACE.*

RIGHT: *A VIEW OF THE PARK CREATED AT THE BEGINNING OF THE NINETEENTH CENTURY BY PETER JOSEPH LENNÉ.* BELOW: *THE ITALIAN GARDENS, WITH AGAVES, PALMS AND ORANGES.*

OPPOSITE, ABOVE: *PAVILIONS IN WROUGHT IRON WITH RICH GOLD DECORATIONS FRAME THE FAÇADE OF THE PALACE;* BELOW: *THE CHINESE TEA HOUSE, A CURIOUS BUILDING WITH STUCCOWORK, STATUES AND A MANDARIN HOLDING AN UMBRELLA ON THE AWNING-STYLE ROOF.*

residence of the court gardener and his assistant.

In the neoclassic style, we find Charlottenhof, built between 1826 and 1829 according to the designs of the architect Karl Friedrich Schinkel. Working around the palace, Lenné demonstrated an extraordinary ability to combine different styles: from a typical formal Italian garden to the best example of an English romantic park – groups of stately trees, light undulations of the land, little lakes, islands and surprising panoramas characterise this successful landscape design.

Yet another tribute to the Italian Renaissance garden, much admired during the period in Germany, is the Sicilian Gardens, carried out in 1857 by Lenné again, which lie next to the New Rooms, designed in 1747 as an orangery and then transformed into guest rooms between 1771 and 1774.

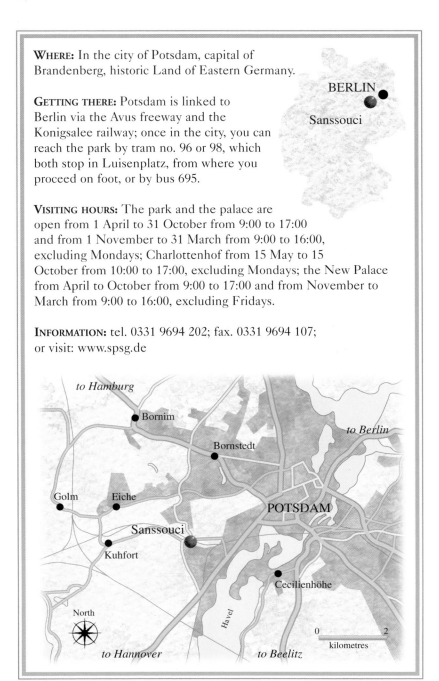

WHERE: In the city of Potsdam, capital of Brandenberg, historic Land of Eastern Germany.

GETTING THERE: Potsdam is linked to Berlin via the Avus freeway and the Konigsalee railway; once in the city, you can reach the park by tram no. 96 or 98, which both stop in Luisenplatz, from where you proceed on foot, or by bus 695.

VISITING HOURS: The park and the palace are open from 1 April to 31 October from 9:00 to 17:00 and from 1 November to 31 March from 9:00 to 16:00, excluding Mondays; Charlottenhof from 15 May to 15 October from 10:00 to 17:00, excluding Mondays; the New Palace from April to October from 9:00 to 17:00 and from November to March from 9:00 to 16:00, excluding Fridays.

INFORMATION: tel. 0331 9694 202; fax. 0331 9694 107; or visit: www.spsg.de

The parterre in the Lower Garden (Het Loo, Holland)

36

FREYR *On the banks of the Meuse, Freÿr's green labyrinths, fountains and ancient orange trees sit at the foot of the sweet slopes of the Ardennes.*

Impeccable lawns, yews planted in quincunx arrangements, fountain basins rippling from water jets, avenues winding between the stern green walls formed from the perfectly trimmed foliage of linden and hornbeam trees – an atmosphere of peace and serenity characterizes the sober, meticulous garden of Freÿr. Set between the course of the Meuse and the wild, inviolate woods of the Ardennes, the garden lies in the heart of an estate that has remained firmly in the hands of one family for twenty generations. The man responsible for the layout of the garden was Guillaume de Beaufort-Spontin, a canon of the Cathedral of Namur, who in 1760 wished to embellish his summer residence. This was a powerful Renaissance stone building, developed around a spacious inner courtyard – a green ornament to his ecclesiastic calling, but also appropriate to the social status of the family, recently risen in the hierarchy of noble titles.

Casting aside the modest flowerbeds and medicinal plants that had framed the castle for more than two centuries, Count Guillaume chose a design in which, without ostentation and unnecessary excesses, the principles of classic French gardens were scrupulously observed: a level space, crossed by a narrow avenue laid out exactly along the principal axis of the building, with a sober parterre arranged in the area closest to the castle. The ruling principle of using only small, well trimmed plants for the decoration of parterres was pushed to the extreme: the large, relatively bare square area that opens at the foot of the castle has only four simple water basins built into stretches of lawn, which are cut into geometric forms.

French design anticipated the need for elements that prevented one from taking in the garden at a single glance, thus retaining the curiosity of visitors. This prescript was observed at Freÿr in the area immediately next to the parterre, where a group of yew trees, planted in a rigorously symmetrical design, weave their branches to form sinuous green bands through which one can glimpse another, English, parterre: a view of carpet-like lawns, and two long water basins parallel to the central avenue – each decorated with precious orange trees. These fifty specimens, arranged along the borders of the

OPPOSITE, TOP: *AERIAL VIEW OF THE CASTLE AND THE GARDEN OF FREŸR;* BOTTOM: *IN THE FOREGROUND, YEW TREES ARRANGED IN STRICT SYMMETRY WEAVE THEIR BRANCHES TO FORM SINUOUS GREEN BANDS. IN THE BACKGROUND, THE SQUARES FORMED BY TALL HEDGEROWS OF PERFECTLY TRIMMED YEWS AND HORNBEAMS TRACE THE PATHS OF THE LABYRINTH.* ABOVE: *ORANGE TREES IN THE* CAISSES DE VERSAILLES *SQUARE, WOODEN VASES.* TOP: *THE WATER BASIN AT THE CENTRE OF THE SQUARES OF YEW AND HORNBEAM TREES.*

flowerbeds at regular intervals, include several that are now 300 years old and were sent to Freÿr, against all odds, from the greenhouses of Stanislao Leczinsky, the King of Polond who was exiled in Nancy.

In the formal gardens of the seventeenth and eighteenth centuries, citrus trees, with their shiny, evergreen leaves, fragrant flowers and radiant colours, had become very popular. They owed their appeal to the legendary Golden Age, and in the grey, cold areas of continental Europe, their presence quietly testified the wealth of their owners and their owners' ability to overcome natural limitations. Even today, the old orange trees of Freÿr are considered the true attraction of the garden, cultivated in *caisses de Versailles* – square vases made of wood to reduce weight and to facilitate their transport – exactly as they were in the times of the canonical Guillaume. Every year, in the oldest orangeries of the Low Countries, these trees are sheltered on 15 October and brought back into the open on 15 May.

On the death of Guillaume in 1766, the estate was inherited by his brother Philippe, who by exploiting grounds with a light slope, made the garden bigger, designing a new, grassy axis perpendicular to the central axis and a scenic labyrinth alongside it: eight squares of

yews and hornbeams contain 6 kilometres of paths, which form fantastic, yet always strictly geometric, shapes.

To complete the garden, a rococo-styled belvedere was built at the highest point in 1785. The spiral decorations and stuccowork on the interior were executed by the Moretti brothers, two esteemed Italian artists, and are still perfectly preserved today.

ABOVE: *THE FIFTY ORANGE TREES ARE BROUGHT INTO THE OPEN AROUND THE MIDDLE OF MAY AND ARE SHELTERED ON 15 OCTOBER IN THE ORANGERIES. SOME OF THESE PLANTS ARE 300 YEARS OLD.*
OPPOSITE, TOP: *THE FRÉDÉRIC SALLE IS AN ELEGANT PAVILION IN THE ROCOCO STYLE BUILT IN 1785 ON THE OCCASION OF THE VISIT OF ONE OF THE DAUGHTERS OF THE EMPRESS MARIA THERESA OF AUSTRIA, THE ARCH DUCHESS MARIA CHRISTINA. THE INTERIOR IS DECORATED WITH SPIRALS AND STUCCOWORK BY THE MORETTI BROTHERS, TWO ITALIANS WHO AT THE TIME WERE VERY ACTIVE IN THE ARISTOCRATIC HOMES OF THE REGION.* OPPOSITE, BOTTOM: *A ROW OF YEW TREES.*

WHERE:
The castle and the gardens of Freÿr are situated on the banks of the Meuse, about 6 kilometres south of Dinant.

GETTING THERE: From Dinant, by car take road no. 96 for Givet; by bus; or by ferry along the Meuse.

VISITING HOURS: From April to September, there are guided tours of the castle and the gardens on Saturday, Sunday and on holidays from 11:00 to 16:00; in July and August there are tours on holidays, except on Monday.

INFORMATION: tel. 0032 82 222200; fax. 0032 82 228323; e-mail: info@freyr.be

BRUSSELS

Freÿr

North

Bouvines-sur-Meuse

to Brussels

DINANT

to Lille

N° 97

to Liegi

Anseremme

Freÿr

Lesse

to Charleville-Mézières

N° 96

Mosa

Falmignoul

0   2
kilometres

KALMTHOUT
One of the most important arboreta in Europe, boasting around 7,000 tree and ornamental shrub specimens.

In the world of gardening, a true marriage between scientific interest and aesthetic talent is rare, and yet it is perhaps the greatest merit of the Kalmthout arboretum. Here, within a well designed green area, one can admire one of the best collections of trees and ornamental shrubs in Europe, with hundreds of roses; more than 600 varieties of azaleas, rhododendrons and magnolias; flowering cherry and apple trees and Japanese maples – in all around 7,000 specimens belonging to 210 species.

The arboretum started to take shape in 1856, when Charles van Geert decided to remove his tiny plant nursery from the centre of Antwerp to Kalmthout. Interested in the unusual botanical species

that plant collectors of the period were discovering in the remotest corners of the Far East and the American continent, Van Geert was looking for a space where he could establish whether the new arrivals would survive the rigours of the Belgian climate when planted out in the open – a fact that was important to establish before selling those exotic marvels as garden plants. Kalmthout seemed to be the ideal solution, because the one-and-a-half-hectare grounds were large enough and the acidity levels of the soil permitted the cultivation of *Ericacea* and conifers, his favourite plants.

The process of acclimatisation bore the desired fruit and in only a few years, to the delight of garden owners in search of rare species,

LEFT: *ONE OF THE EXOTIC TREES AT HOME IN KALMTHOUT: THE* CORNUS KOUSA *FROM KOREA AND JAPAN. IT HAS SMALL GREEN FLOWERS, ENVELOPED WITH EYE-CATCHING WHITE BRACT (MODIFIED LEAVES).* BELOW: KALMIA LATIFOLI, *A BUSY SHRUB FROM THE UNITED STATES.*

ABOVE: *THE ROSE VARIETY, 'TOBY TRISTAM'.* OPPOSITE: *THE COUNTRY HOUSE, VEILED IN RHODODENDRONS, WHICH IS REACHED ALONG AN AVENUE FLANKED WITH CONIFERS THAT ARE AT LEAST 150 YEARS OLD.* OPPOSITE, TOP: *'RUSH' ROSES, A FLOURISHING, FRAGRANT VARIETY.*

43

Van Geert's catalogue was enriched with Hostas, golden maples, Japanese pines, American hydrangias, oriental hellebores: a long list of plants that had never before been seen in Europe, and that were available at Kalmthout before any other western nursery.

On the wave of this success, an even more exciting period began for Kalmthout at the end of the nineteenth century. The nursery was bought by Antoine Kort, an enterprising horticulturalist who stepped

LEFT: A GLIMPSE OF THE ARBORETUM, WHERE TREES, SHRUBS AND HERBACEOUS PLANTS ARE ARRANGED TO ENTICE THE GAZE. ABOVE: A GROUP OF FOXGLOVES. RIGHT: PICEA ABIES 'CRANSTONII'. OPPOSITE, BOTTOM: CORNUS CONTROVERSA, 'PAGODA', A SMALL TREE FROM CHINA AND JAPAN WITH CREAM-COLOURED COROLLAS WHEN IN FLOWER IN MAY AND PURPLE LEAVES IN THE AUTUMN.

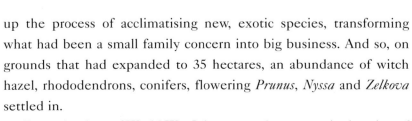

up the process of acclimatising new, exotic species, transforming what had been a small family concern into big business. And so, on grounds that had expanded to 35 hectares, an abundance of witch hazel, rhododendrons, conifers, flowering *Prunus*, *Nyssa* and *Zelkova* settled in.

From the time of World War I, however, the economic situation of the nursery started to deteriorate. The era of great parks was over and the demand for large ornamental trees had fallen drastically throughout all of Europe. During World War II commercial activity stopped entirely – soon the nursery was abandoned.

But in the 1950s, the brothers Georges and Robert De Belder, two wealthy diamond importers who were also enthusiastic botanists, and Robert's wife, a Slovenian landscape artist named Jelena Kovacic, arrived to save this extraordinary collection of rare plants from an

ABOVE: *A GROUP OF OLD CONIFERS.* RIGHT: *CLUSTERS OF FLOWERS FROM* PRUNUS LUSITANICA, *COMMONLY KNOWN AS* PORTUGUESE CHERRY. *FAR RIGHT: A DENSE LITTLE TREE WITH EVERGREEN LEAVES, REACHING A HEIGHT OF UP TO 6 METRES, FROM SPAIN AND PORTUGAL. OPPOSITE, TOP: THE FRENCH WINDOWS OF THE COUNTRY HOUSE, WHICH OPEN ONTO THE GREEN.*

ignominious end. From the ashes of the old nursery, with taste and professional competence, they gave birth to a wonderful garden. After tearing down unhealthy plants and substituting them with hundreds of rare species from all parts of the globe, Jelena abandoned the sensible arrangements of traditional gardens, preferring to organise this prestigious collection in a series of informal flowerbeds laid around the feet of the large trees planted by Van Geert and Kort. She combined forms, colours and textures in new ways and then softened the whole by creating expansive lawns and wide grassy avenues.

In this way, thanks to the De Belder family, Kalmthout became a beautiful garden in every season. In spring it is fresh and delicate with flowering *Prunus*, apple, many varieties of magnolias, and a long list of azaleas and rhododendrons. In summer the roses, fuschsias and herbaceous plants are at their best. This is the season in which the splendid inflorescence of *Hydrangea paniculata* 'Grandiflora' blends with the snow-white clouds of agapanthus and the grey-green, pale-cream colours of *Macleaya cordata* to create a lovely white garden. In autumn, the majestic evergreen conifers create a spectacular contrast with the orange, red and yellow leaves of the Japanese maples, the azaleas from Ghent, and the oaks, ferns and witch hazels. Stretches of white, pink and mauve meadow saffron appear, thousands of small red fruits mature on the branches of flowering apples, and shiny purple berries sparkle on *Phytolacca americana*. The garden does not lose its attractions in the

winter either, thanks to the weave of naked branches, the glossy mahogany trunks of maples, the silvery trunks of birches, and the spectacular flowerings of a substantial collection of witch hazels – one of the glories of Kalmthout.

Today the arboretum belongs to the province of Antwerp, but occupies a smaller area than it did in the times of Kort – only 12 hectares. However, it seems infinitely larger thanks to the careful layout of the flowerbeds, which change as you view them from different angles. In the garden you will also find two lakes surrounded by aceas and aquatic plants; a delightful pavilion draped with ivy and variegated leaves; and a country house surrounded by old rhododendrons, which you reach along an avenue flanked with majestic conifers planted one and a half centuries ago by Van Geert.

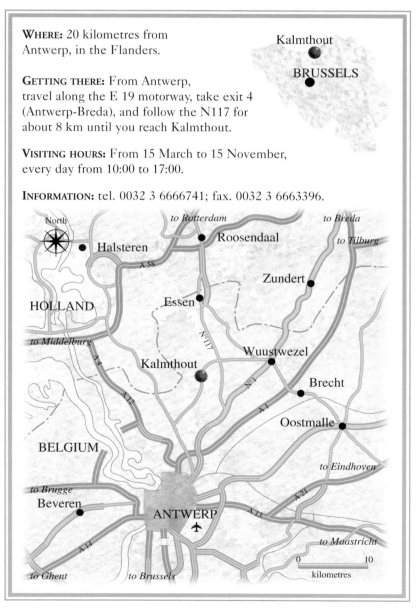

WHERE: 20 kilometres from Antwerp, in the Flanders.

GETTING THERE: From Antwerp, travel along the E 19 motorway, take exit 4 (Antwerp-Breda), and follow the N117 for about 8 km until you reach Kalmthout.

VISITING HOURS: From 15 March to 15 November, every day from 10:00 to 17:00.

INFORMATION: tel. 0032 3 6666741; fax. 0032 3 6663396.

HET LOO *A sumptuous baroque garden returned to the splendours of the eighteenth century after a twenty-four-year restoration.*

In 1684, Prince William III of Orange, recently nominated 'Stadtholder' of the Province of Gheldria, decided to build a country residence near Veluwe, an area without trees yet rich in game, and therefore ideal for hunting on horseback – his favourite sport. When the building was entrusted to the Dutch architect, Jacob Roman, and the French decorator, Daniel Marot, and began in the spring of 1685, Prince William and his wife, Mary, daughter of James II of England, followed it with interest. It took only four years to build the comfortable palace overlooking the wide green space known as the Lower Garden. Here principles derived from André Le Nôtre's park of Versailles, which had become the model to follow at all costs – were woven into the more sober Dutch traditions.

The rectangular shape of the garden, modest in relation to the proportions of Versailles, was divided in two parts symmetrically arranged in relation to the central axis, and enclosed by a transversal avenue flanked by four rows of oaks at the bottom. In keeping with the style of the period, the geometric rigour of the layout was observed in minute detail and plants modelled by hand refused to concede the unpredictability of nature: the eight square parterres were decorated with a complex embroidery of boxwood and bordered with flowers planted at equidistant points from one another to enhance their value, instead of being massed together as they were in French gardens.

To give the garden a vertical dimension, the key points of the layout were accentuated with gilded lead or white marble statues immortalising mythological figures. Junipers and yews were trimmed into pyramidal shapes and arranged at regular distances, while the murmur of fountains introduced a sonorous element to the garden. The Venus Fountain, along the central axis, was flanked on either side by the unusual Globe Fountain – a gushing copper sphere painted blue and yellow with engravings of the four corners of the earth – and by the Fountain of Heavenly Spheres, which represented each sign of the zodiac as they appeared in the skies on 30 April 1662, the birthday of Princess Mary in London.

At Het Loo, the fountains functioned day and night by means of an

RIGHT AND OPPOSITE: IN THE PARTERRE FLOWERBEDS OF THE LOWER GARDEN, THE BOXWOOD HEDGEROWS FORM CURLS AND SPIRALS ON THE COLOURED GRAVEL. ABOVE: THE COPPER GLOBE FOUNTAIN PAINTED IN YELLOW AND BLUE, REPRESENTING THE FOUR CORNERS OF THE EARTH.

*The present gardens of Het Loo are a faithful reproduction of those created in the second half of the seventeenth century – an exceptional reconstruction made possible by the detailed accounts inspired by the gardens, especially those of Walter Harris, William's personal physician. Harris described the enlargements and embellishments of the garden to Queen Mary, who after ascending the throne of England, could no longer find time to return to her beloved Het Loo. As a result of this precious information, it was possible to reconstruct the elaborate designs of the parterres with the utmost precision. The flowering plants arranged in the borders were exactly those used in the baroque gardens at the end of the seventeenth century. The statues, some authentic, others reproductions made from synthetic resin, were repositioned at the exact points chosen by Jacob Roman and Daniel Marot. Even the fountains and the colonnade at the bottom of the garden are exact replicas of those that appeared in the original plans. The meticulous and expensive reconstruction of Het Loo also uncovered many archaeological treasures under a thick layer of earth added during the period of Louis Bonaparte. The walls on the sides of the garden were recovered with stone of identical form, size and colour to that found in the course of the excavations. To make room for the parterres, it was necessary to fell most of the trees planted during the course of the nineteenth and twentieth centuries – a difficult but inevitable decision, which only preserved a few precious specimens, like a Canadian maple in the King's Garden, and a tulip tree (*Liriodendron tulipifera*) and two red beech trees in the Upper Garden.*

ingenious hydraulic system designed for the mills of Veluwe. Water was drawn from underground and conveyed to various points in the garden across a network of small canals – a coup in relation to the Grand Palace of Versailles, where the scarcity of available water – stagnant and with a rather unpleasant odour – only permitted gardeners to activate the fountains along the walking route of the king and his courtiers.

The Lower Garden was enclosed with walls 4 metres high, distancing itself from the Dutch tradition, which habitually surrounded green spaces with canals. The walls were an innovation precipitated by the need to protect the garden from the sand raised by strong winds in the area. They also encouraged the construction of long, raised terraces close to the walls, ideal observation points from which to admire the elaborate design of the parterres.

In addition to the Lower Garden, as a specific tribute to the glory of the Prince as well as a place to receive guests, Roman and Marot created two private gardens on the sides of the palace, next to the royal couple's apartments. In that of the king, divided in two parts, there were three parterres decorated with boxwood arabesques and surrounded by borders of red and blue flowers (the colours of the Orange-Nassau family), and a large bowling green for William and his retinue to play bowls or croquet.

In the garden designed for the queen on the other side of the palace, hornbeam pergolas formed a network of green corridors for relaxing walks in the shade on hot summer days. They emphasised the close and intimate character of the area, which contained fountains

TOP: *THE QUEEN'S PRIVATE GARDEN. IN GOOD WEATHER IT HOUSED POTTED CITRUS TREES, POMEGRANATES, OLIVES, FIGS AND OTHER PLANTS UNCOMMON IN THE LATITUDES OF HET LOO.* LEFT: *THE LONG CENTRAL AVENUE AND THE PALACE.* ABOVE: *YEWS AND JUNIPERS TRIMMED INTO CONICAL AND PYRAMIDAL SHAPES, STATUES AND CLIMBERS GIVE THE GARDEN A VERTICAL DIMENSION.* OPPOSITE: *A VIEW OF THE LOWER GARDEN, WITH THE VENUS FOUNTAIN AT THE CENTRE, AS WELL AS THE UPPER GARDEN, ENCLOSED BY A SEMI-CIRCULAR COLONNADE AND THE KING'S FOUNTAIN.*

51

ABOVE: *THE KING'S FOUNTAIN, THE PRINCIPAL ATTRACTION OF THE UPPER GARDEN, WITH THE STATELY COLONNADE BEHIND IT. OCTAGONAL IN SHAPE, ITS WATER JET RISES UP TO 13 METRES IN THE AIR. IN FRONT OF THE WATER BASIN ARE ELEGANT GRASS PARTERRES AND SEVERAL TREES THAT WERE PLANTED IN THE NINETEENTH CENTURY, WHEN THE GARDENS OF HET LOO WERE COMPLETELY REDESIGNED TO SUIT THE LANDSCAPE STYLE THEN IN FASHION. LEFT: THE VENUS FOUNTAIN AT THE CENTRE OF THE LOWER GARDEN. BELOW: THE DOLPHIN FOUNTAIN.*

Known and admired in all of Europe, the gardeners of Het Loo preserved their formal layout up until the middle of the nineteenth century, when the Upper Garden was replaced with a landscape design by the court architect, Philip Schonck. Then began a period of decline, signalled by weeds invading the flowerbeds and the theft of statues – to which Louis Bonaparte, nominated King of Holland from 1806 to 1810, fortunately put an end. In a drastic intervention, the architect Alexandre Dufour eliminated parterres, knocked down terraces and boundary walls, levelled the grounds and transformed the garden into a vast landscape park.

The last chapter in the history of Het Loo began in 1970, with the decision to transform the complex into a museum, and ended in 1984, when – after the eradication of nineteenth and twentieth century modifications and a scrupulous, costly restoration – the palace and gardens regained their original appearance and were opened to the public.

ABOVE: *ONE OF THE TWO CASCADES OF NARCISSUS, ARRANGED SYMMETRICALLY IN THE LOWER GARDEN AND RECONSTRUCTED WITH THE DISCOVERY OF ORIGINAL FRAGMENTS. IN THE FOREGROUND, ONE OF THE CANALS THAT FEED THE FOUNTAIN.*

WHERE: The palace and gardens of Het Loo lie in the north of Apeldoorn, a city 25 kilometres north of Arnhem.

GETTING THERE: From Apeldoorn take bus no. 102 or 104.

VISITING HOURS: The gardens are open all year round from Tuesday to Sunday, from 10:00 to 17:00. They are closed on New Year's Day.

INFORMATION: tel. 0031 55 5772400; fax. 0031 55 5219983; e-mail: info@paleishetloo.nl; or visit www.hetloo.nl

and flowerbeds decorated with boxwood curls and feminine flowers like lilies and columbines, traditional emblems of the Virgin Mary. In good weather, the gardeners arranged vases of citrus trees, pomegranates, olives, myrtles, figs and oleanders: precious plants in those times and in those latitudes.

In 1689, when William and his wife were crowned sovereigns of England, the list of initiatives to celebrate their growth in power included the decision to enlarge Het Loo. To the north of the garden, beyond the transverse avenues flanked by oak trees, a new, slightly raised area was added. The Upper Garden, as it was named, was enclosed by a stately semi-circular colonnade and decorated with elegant grass parterres symmetrically arranged to balance the lengthening of the central axis. But the show piece in this area was the spectacular King's Fountain, an octagonal marble basin 32 metres wide with a water jet that rises up to 13 metres – a technical marvel for the period.

EASTERN EUROPE

*LAZIENKI
PARK
(WARSAW,
POLAND)*

WALLENSTEIN *Echoes of Italian styles are found in the garden of Albrecht von Wallenstein, a military man with a love of flowers.*

The Bohemian Duke Albrecht Wenzel Eusebius von Wallenstein, who lived between the sixteenth and seventeenth centuries, had two great passions: the army and gardening. To satisfy the first, he had actively participated in the Thirty Years War in the service of the Habsburgs, defeating the protestant forces at Dessau, forcing the retreat of Christian IV of Denmark, and then leading the imperial army against the troops of Gustav IV Adolf of Sweden.

To satisfy the second, his love of greenery, he built two magnificent gardens, one in the Bohemian countryside and one at Prague. The latter, still well preserved, was created to dignify an immense and sumptuous palace built between 1623 and 1630 at a stone's throw from the Moldava River – among the General's more ambitious dreams, it hoped to compete with the royal castle. To realise this grandiose project, Wallenstein did not hesitate to raze twenty-five homes and a number of shops and warehouses to the ground. He had entrusted the design of the new palace and garden to a team of architects led by Giovanni Pieroni, a Florentine raised in the court of the De' Medici family and a student of Galileo Galilei, who proposed many elements from Italian villas of the period for the Bohemian capital. For example, an elegant portico with three arches embellished with stuccowork and frescoes, inspired by the main façade of the palace, provided a harmonious link between the interior space of the home and the exterior space of the garden.

The Italian style is also evident in the layout of the green space that opens in front of the portico: a square parterre, enclosed by high hornbeam walls and divided by two avenues that intersect at right angles to form four symmetrical flowerbeds. Each of these is decorated with low, boxwood hedgerows that form four geometric compartments for narcissuses, tulips and other flowering plants. Where the two avenues intersect, the parterre has also been embellished by a marble basin and statue of *Venus and Cupid*, as well as other bronze mythological figures commissioned from the Dutch sculptor, Adriaen de Vries. At the end of the Thirty Year War, the statues were confiscated by the Swedish troops and taken to the Palace of Drottningholm: a posthumous retaliation against the once bellicose master of the house, and a loss that was remedied in the early years of the twentieth century by a series of identical reproductions. To further complement the fountains and sculptures (wisely positioned at the bottom of the avenues to enhance the views), Wallenstein also introduced an aviary. This large, elegant construction, with its precious fittings, hedges, shrubs and trees for exotic birds to nest in, is still in perfect condition today.

In the garden right in front of the stables, Pieroni created a wide stretch of water with a small artificial island in the centre to carry a statue of Hercules battling with a dragon. This decoration had a famous precedent in the great basin designed almost a century before by Niccolò Pericoli (il Tribolo) for

OPPOSITE, TOP: *THE ISLAND IN FRONT OF THE STABLES, WITH ITS STATUE OF HERCULES BATTLING A DRAGON;* BOTTOM: *THE BOXWOOD PARTERRE. STATUES OF MYTHOLOGICAL FIGURES* (LEFT, APOLLO) *ON THE SIDES OF THE CENTRAL AVENUE ARE REPRODUCTIONS OF THOSE CREATED IN THE SEVENTEENTH CENTURY AND CONFISCATED BY THE SWEDES AT THE END OF THE THIRTY YEAR WAR.* TOP: *DETAIL OF A FOUNTAIN.*

LEFT: *BEHIND THE FISH FOUNTAIN IS THE WALL OF STALACTITES THAT SURROUNDS THE GARDEN, HOUSES A LARGE ARTIFICIAL GROTTO AND IS MADE OF BLOCKS OF TRAVERTINE MARBLE* (DETAIL BELOW).

OPPOSITE, ABOVE: *DETAIL OF THE PARTERRE. THE PERFECTLY TRIMMED BOXWOOD HEDGEROWS LINE GEOMETRIC FLOWERBEDS CONTAINING TULIPS AND OTHER FLOWERS IN SEASON;* BOTTOM: *FOUNTAIN OF HERCULES AND SAGITTARIUS.*

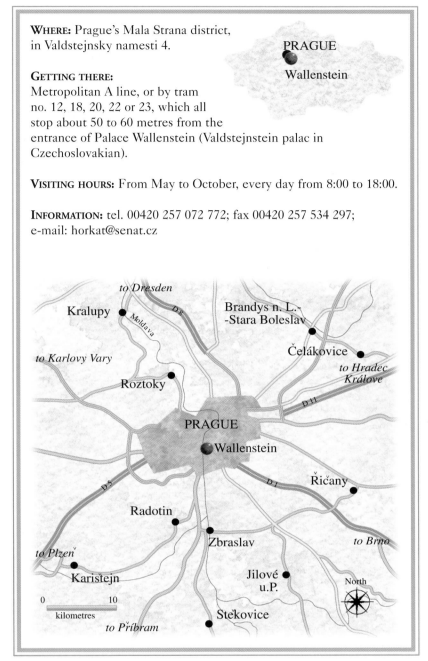

WHERE: Prague's Mala Strana district, in Valdstejnsky namesti 4.

GETTING THERE:
Metropolitan A line, or by tram no. 12, 18, 20, 22 or 23, which all stop about 50 to 60 metres from the entrance of Palace Wallenstein (Valdstejnstein palac in Czechoslovakian).

VISITING HOURS: From May to October, every day from 8:00 to 18:00.

INFORMATION: tel. 00420 257 072 772; fax 00420 257 534 297; e-mail: horkat@senat.cz

the garden of the Villa Medicea di Castello, and then reproduced at Boboli and at other grand Italian residences. The enormous artificial grotto dug out of the garden's perimeter wall brings to mind those that ancient Roman emperors created in their villas to amaze and entertain their guests, and that many centuries later were rediscovered and reused by Italian Renaissance architects. These were fantastic and mysterious places, where the walls were covered with stalactites and artificial rocks made with glass fragments, coral branches and shells from distant shores. These were settings enveloped by shade and ruled by water, which dripped from delicate little tubes, or gushed unexpectedly over unfortunate guests. Here the master of the house could retreat on sultry summer days to bathe, lunch with friends, or rest in the cool of the evening.

LAZIENKI PARK *This green space serves as a reminder of a great past, and is today a reference point for the townsfolk of Warsaw.*

Lazienki Park, which covers an area of 76 hectares and houses a series of extraordinary buildings as well as plants, lakes and lawns, assumed its current appearance after a series of adjustments and embellishments commissioned by its many famous proprietors over the course of the centuries. This began with Queen Bona Sforza, wife of Zygmunt Stary, who in 1548 ordered the building of a large wooden castle in the heart of what was then the dense and beautiful forest of Ujazdow.

During this period, the famous Castle of Bona was surrounded by an elegant Italian garden, where in good weather, festivities, recitals and performances of every kind were organised. Captured by the beauty of the place, in 1624, King Sigismondo III replaced the old wooden castle with a new, more solid edifice. This had a square layout that imitated the forms of Italian fortresses, with four imposing hexagonal donjons in each corner. The King also decided to surround the grounds that descended towards the Vistula River with a palisade to create a zoological park with bisons, bears, boars, fallow deer, and other wild animals, which his guests could securely observe from the height of a tower.

In 1683 the ownership of Ujazdow passed to Prince Stanislao Lubomirski, Crown Marshall, who encharged the architect Tylman van Gameren with rearranging the interior rooms of the castle and designing a new garden in the formal French style, which was in high fashion in all of Europe at the time. This design featured canals and geometrically shaped water basins, orderly boskets surrounded by hedgerows, and straight avenues radiating from clearings. Prince Stanislao also asked the

architect Van Gameren to design a few garden pavilions. One of these, the luxurious Bath House, not only gave its name to the whole complex (*lazienki* means bath), but formed the nucleus of the famous Palace on the Water that would be built in the following century. Surrounded by canals and stretches of water, and decorated with extraordinary stuccowork representing scenes from Ovid's *Metamorphoses*, this building contains a large bathroom where the Master of the House enjoyed relaxing with his friends after a hard day's work.

The most important chapter in the history of the park began in 1764, the year that signalled the beginning of the reign of Stanislao August Poniatowski. After having bought the Ujazdow Castle, the last sovereign of Poland also wanted to enlarge and enhance it to transform it into his official residence: a dream that unfortunately he did not fulfill because of the expense involved. He therefore had to be content with establishing Ujazdow as his private residence, transforming the old zoological park and the French-styled garden into an original English landscape park, furnished with a large group of extraordinary buildings. This slow metamorphosis – lasting more than 20 years and sustained by talented artists like the architect, Domenico Merlini, the sculptor André Le Brun, and the painter Jan Bogumil Plersch – finally gave birth to an absolutely extraordinary interweaving of architecture and landscape design.

A wide road, 5 kilometres long, was laid down between two rows of trees and the scenic Royal Walk was designed: a straight avenue flanked by two streams of water and wooden trellises covered with the interweaving branches of *Robinia*

ABOVE: *THE UNUSUAL THEATRE, WHICH IMITATES THE STRUCTURE OF A GREEK AUDITORIUM AND WHICH LIES ON AN ISLET IN A LARGE LAKE. IT WAS BUILT BY JOHANN BAPTIST KAMSETZER BETWEEN 1790 AND 1791. IN 1904, THE MONUMENT DEDICATED TO FRÉDÉRIC CHOPIN* (OPPOSITE) *WAS CREATED BY WACLAW SZYMANOWSKI, AROUND WHICH FAMOUS CONCERT PIANISTS OFTEN PERFORM THE WORKS OF THE GREAT COMPOSER* (RIGHT AND OPPOSITE, TOP).

PLANNED AND LAID OUT IN HOMAGE TO THE CANON OF LANDSCAPE DESIGN, THE PARK IS THE WORK OF J. C. SCHUCH, AN ARCHITECT FROM DRESDEN, WHO GAINED INSPIRATION BY VISITING THE MOST FAMOUS GARDENS OF FRANCE, HOLLAND AND ENGLAND. SPREAD OUT OVER AN AREA OF 73 HECTARES, THE PARK IS TODAY ONE OF THE MOST FAMILIAR AND FREQUENTED OF THE CITY OF WARSAW.

psudoacacia. The old canals were transformed into 'natural' streams flowing among groups of horse chestnut, poplars, and alternating fir and larch trees, while the geometric water basins around the Bath House were replaced by a large lake with irregular banks covered with flowers and shrubs.

Gradually this immense park became further populated by architectural jewels, like the White House, a rococo building with delightful floral frescoes that the king had designed for his lover. Or the old orangery, with its baroque theatre, containing miraculously preserved decorations created by Merlini and Plersch, and the unusual amphitheatre on an island in the middle of a lake, where a stretch of water separates the audience from the stage.

And then came the most important building in the park, enlarged and enhanced from the old Bath House to develop its role appropriately as the new residence of the king – the neoclassic palace, which forms a reflection in the water of the lake. Crowned by an attic decorated with statues, it consists of a series of sumptuous rooms, like the Ball Room,

63

decorated with stuccowork, frescoes and reproductions of the *Hercules Farnese* and *Apollo Belvedere* statues. Or the Rotonda, that recalls the interior of the Pantheon, with its dome-shaped ceiling supported by a circular row of corinthian columns. Or indeed the graceful and intimate Dining Room, famous for the Thursday breakfasts, when the best intellectuals of the period would gather around the king's table.

After being set on fire by German troops at the end of World War II, the Palace on the Water was immediately restored, and together with other eighteenth-century buildings that had not been damaged, it became an independent section of the National Museum, housing precious collections of paintings and sculptures. The immense and picturesque greenery surrounding the Palace has preserved its landscape design and is today the favourite public garden for inhabitants of Warsaw taking their Sunday walk.

ABOVE AND OPPOSITE, TOP: *THE PALACE ON THE WATER, THE MOST IMPORTANT BUILDING IN THE PARK AND ONE OF THE MOST BEAUTIFUL OF WARSAW. BUILT IN 1683–1690, IT WAS REWORKED IN 1775–1776 BY DOMENICO MERLINI, WHO CREATED THE FAÇADE WITH ITS CLASSIC PRONAOS. LEFT: THE EGYPTIAN TEMPLE, WHICH WAS THE WORK OF JAKOB KUBICKI IN 1820.*

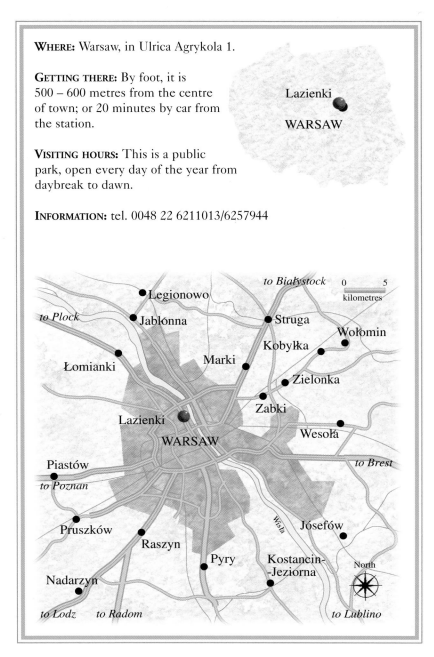

WHERE: Warsaw, in Ulrica Agrykola 1.

GETTING THERE: By foot, it is 500 – 600 metres from the centre of town; or 20 minutes by car from the station.

VISITING HOURS: This is a public park, open every day of the year from daybreak to dawn.

INFORMATION: tel. 0048 22 6211013/6257944

Lazienki

WARSAW

to Białystok

0   5
kilometres

Legionowo

to Plock   Jablónna

Struga

Wołomin

Kobyłka

Łomianki   Marki

Zielonka

Zabki

Lazienki

Wesoła

WARSAW

Piastów

to Brest

to Poznan

Wisła   Jósefów

Pruszków

Raszyn   Pyry   Kostancin-
-Jeziorna   North

Nadarzyn

to Lodz   to Radom   to Lublino

VILLA SZECHENYI *A baroque jewel created by the Count who loved modernity.*
ESTERHAZA *The residence that immortalised the power of a legendary prince.*

Impassioned by progress and technological developments, the Magyar Count Istvàn Széchenyi did his best to promote the modernization of Hungary in the first half of the nineteenth century. The Count founded the National Academy of Sciences, and was responsible for building the first bridge to join Buda and Pest on the Danube, starting steamship navigation on Lake Balaton, and expanding the national railway.

The indefatigable Count also adopted an enlightened attitude to the running of Nagycenk, an estate that had belonged to his family for two centuries. Here he introduced modern breeding techniques for race horses, importing stallions and mares from England. Among the best contributions to the elegant palace built in the eighteenth century at the centre of the estate was the installation of an innovative ventilated airspace under the floors to reduce humidity and, before for the rest of Hungary, gas and light installations and toilet facilities with running water.

Improvements and novelties were also in store for the garden, which Count Istvàn wanted to modernise, placing an English-style park – with undulating lawns, majestic trees and winding lanes – next to the decidedly formal parterre created in the eighteenth century in

RIGHT: *THE PARTERRE IN FRONT OF THE MAIN FAÇADE OF THE VILLA SZÉCHENYI. CREATED IN THE EIGHTEENTH CENTURY, IT CONSISTS OF SIX FLOWERBEDS, IN WHICH THE BOXWOOD HEDGEROWS FORM SUMPTUOUS ARABESQUES. THE FLOWERBEDS ARE ARRANGED SYMMETRICALLY ALONG THE SIDES OF A CENTRAL AVENUE BORDERED BY CONE-SHAPED YEWS. ABOVE: A RESTING POINT IN THE ENGLISH-STYLE PARK. OPPOSITE, TOP: A VIEW OF THE EIGHTEENTH-CENTURY PALACE.*

ABOVE: *THE FOUNTAIN SITUATED IN THE CENTRAL AVENUE OF THE PARTERRE, NEAR THE MAIN ENTRANCE OF THE ESTATE.* RIGHT: *THE GLASSHOUSE, BUILT IN 1860, AND DAMAGED IN WORLD WAR II. RESTORATIONS WERE COMPLETED IN 1988.* OPPOSITE: *THE PARK.*

WHERE: Villa Széchenyi is in Nagycenk, 12 kilometres from Sopron. Estherhaza is in Fertöd, 30 kilometres from Sopron.

GETTING THERE: By car from Sopron take highway 84 until you reach Nagycenk, from where you can continue to Fertöd along highway 85. You can also reach Nagycenk by train or bus from Sopron. There is a bus service linking Fertöd to Sopron.

VISITING HOURS: Villa Széchenyi is open from 1 April to 31 October, between 10:00 and 18:00 (excluding Mondays); Esterhaza is open from 15 March to 31 October between 10:00 and 18:00 (excluding Mondays) and from 1 November to 14 March, Fridays, Saturdays and Sundays between 10:00 and 16:00.

INFORMATION: Villa Széchenyi, tel. 0036 99 360023; fax. 0036 99 360260; e-mail: nagycenk@gymsmuzeum.hu. Esterhaza, tel. 0036 99 537640; fax. 0036 99 537642; e-mail: eszterhaza@mah.hu

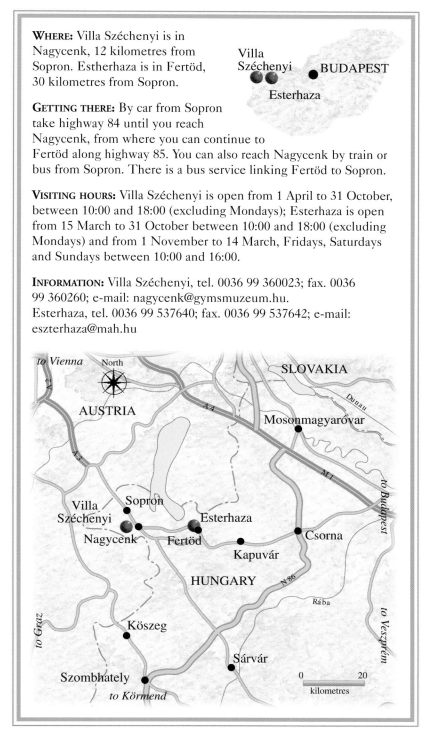

front of the palace façade. This was an elegant, but not overly luxurious, space enclosed by hedgerows in line with the refined moderation of the Széchenyi family: six flowerbeds decorated with enormous boxwood arabesques and vases of flowers were arranged symmetrically on either side of a straight, central avenue, punctuated with yews trimmed into geometric forms and enclosed by a fountain at the bottom. Thanks to the discovery of the original plans, this delicate baroque jewel was rebuilt a few decades ago, repairing the serious damage it suffered during World War II.

ESTERHAZA
The largest and most beautiful baroque mansion in Hungary. The garden is only partly accessible in anticipation of a long and patient restoration that will return it to its earlier splendour.

In the second half of the eighteenth century, the legendary Prince Miklos Esterházy built a residence that was less modern than Villa Széchenyi but definitely more luxurious, in the heart of an estate on the banks of Lake Fertö. It reflected the desire, common among many noblemen of the period, to emulate the splendours of Versailles by designing magnificent palaces and transforming parts of the country-side into scenic formal gardens; ideal and indispensable stages for festivities, receptions and the refined rituals that characterised noble aristocratic life.

For his new home, the worldly and wealthy Esterházy – whose fortune one could measure by one of his formal outfits, studded with diamonds, eliciting admiration and envy in all the courts of Europe – had selected a miserable marsh teeming with insects. Although the area was obviously not fit for the purpose, the Prince would not hear reason, unshakeable in his ambitious decision to defy and bend nature to his will. Canals, dams and dykes were excavated, running up staggering expenses, but finally, in 1788, the new residence, named Esterhaza in honour of the Master of the House, was inaugurated in all its splendour.

The palace, a sumptuous building in the rococo style, looked out onto a vast, French-style park,

supplied, as fashion demanded, with a parterre decorated with yews and boxwood trimmed into geometric shapes, precious orange trees in vases, statues, fountains and flowerbeds that were renewed every month by a group of industrious gardeners. Beyond the parterre there were thick boskets of yews and chestnuts, and compact hornbeam walls outlined avenues that radiated outwards, or enclosed intimate cabinets cleared away among the trees. These were modelled on those of Versailles and provided ideal areas for plays, open-air parties and romantic trysts. It took years to cultivate these extraordinary green walls however, and so

the end of a majestic avenue of chestnut trees and embellished by a staircase adorned with an elaborate wrought iron balustrade and by a host of columns in red, yellow and green marble. Here you could hear the music of Joseph Haydn, a regular guest at Esterhaza, accompanied by an orchestra that was considered among the best in Europe at the time. This broke up immediately after the death of Prince Miklos, in 1790, when the Esterházy family decided to remove to Kismarton to be closer to the court of Vienna. For this luxurious residence, stripped of its furnishings and its precious collection of paintings, a period of inexorable decay began. Further damages were suffered during the course of World War II. The complex is currently undergoing restoration.

to cope with the immediate scenic necessities of an important reception, here, as in other gardens of the period, simple, painted wooden partitions were often used. On the occasion of the Empress Maria Theresa's visit, Prince Milkos laid out an enormous lunch room for 8,000 guests in an oval clearing among the trees, surrounded by panels cut in the form of arches and decorated with leaves and flowers. Among the marvels of the park there was also a series of luxurious pavilions – popular destinations for garden walks – with inlaid walnut floors, frescoes on the walls, gilded couches and agate tables.

Hidden away in a corner, there was an unusual hermitage surrounded by brambles and featuring a statue of a beggar. Then, to host the lively activities of masked balls, an extravagant Chinese Pavilion was planned and, for marionette performances, a theatre in the form of a cave was built. This had a row of niches dug out of the walls, was covered with silk cloth, shells and crystals, and was illuminated by hundreds of lamps.

The real glory of the garden, though, was the opera theatre, placed at

OPPOSITE: *THE TERRACE AT THE FOOT OF THE MAIN PALACE FAÇADE, WHICH YOU ACCESS VIA TWO SYMMETRICALLY ARRANGED STAIRCASES, AND FROM WHERE YOU CAN ENJOY THE VIEW OF THE MAIN COURTYARD. RIGHT: DETAIL OF ONE OF THE LAMPOSTS THAT ILLUMINATE THE STAIRCASES. OPPOSITE, TOP: THE REAR FAÇADE OF THE PALACE, IN FRONT OF WHICH EXTENDS A VAST LAWN DOTTED WITH CONE-SHAPED YEWS (TOP). ABOVE: THE STABLES.*

PETRODVOREC *Statues, fountains and cascades look out over the Baltic Sea from the summer residence of Peter the Great.*

Many historical events accompanied the long evolutionary periods of gardens: in Russia they marked the beginning of a new political course. In the first years of the eighteenth century, Peter the Great decided to initiate a programme of modernisation. His decision to move the capital of Moscow to the new city of St Petersburg was intended as a tangible sign of this transformation: a wide, open window onto Europe. To emphasise his ambitious programme, the Tsar ordered the construction of a series of summer residences in the immediate vicinity of the city. The most significant of these was no doubt Peterhof, or Petrovorec, as it is known today, for which the Tzar planned a garden capable of rivalling Italian, French and Dutch masterpieces, and of showing the world the new face of Russia.

The park is situated on a spectacular natural terrace overlooking the Gulf of Finland. Many talented artists arrived in St Petersburg from all over Europe to work on this project, which began in 1714 and lasted more than ten years, including the architect Jean Baptiste Alexandre Le Blond, an expert in the Italian version of the French style, and Niccolò Michetti, pupil of the great Carlo Fontana.

Although Petrovorec boasts spectacular boskets, which form a vast green belt around the palace (the Tzar, a plant enthusiast, had ordered 40,000 trees: elms and maples from the interior zones of Russia; lime trees, beeches and fruit trees from western Europe), the main feature of the garden is undoubtedly water. It animates a seemingly infinite series of fountains, basins and canals, transported along a complex hydraulic system from water springs more than 20 kilometres away,

LEFT AND OPPOSITE: *IN FRONT OF THE NORTH FAÇADE OF THE GREAT PALACE, A SPECTACULAR CASCADE DESCENDS OVER A SERIES OF WIDE MARBLE STEPS TO THE LOWER GARDENS AND A CENTRAL GROTTO DECORATED BY GILDED BRONZE STATUES. AT ITS FEET IS A CIRCULAR BASIN WHERE SAMSON BATTLES A LION, A 20 METRE JET RISING FROM ITS JAWS. THE SCULPTURE ALLUDES TO THE BATTLE OF POLTAVA IN 1709, DURING WHICH PETER THE GREAT GOT THE BETTER OF THE SWEDISH ARMY. A LONG CANAL LEADS OFF FROM THE FOUNTAIN BASIN TOWARDS THE GULF OF FINLAND. ABOVE: DETAIL OF A GOLDEN CUPOLA ON THE GREAT PALACE.*

and throws itself against the foot of the palace in the form of sea waves: a marvel that no European garden could boast.

Exploiting the shape of the land, the park was laid out on two levels. The Upper Gardens open onto a gigantic courtyard in front of the south façade of the Great Palace, hosting a parterre made up of square lawns bordered with little trees and shrubs trimmed into geometrical forms, and enhanced by fountains and gilded lead statues. On the suggestion of Le Blond, enormous storage basins were built in this area to feed the large number of fountains scattered throughout the 120 hectares of the park. The Lower Gardens,

suspended between the northern façade of the palace and the sea, present an extraordinary theatre of water framed by flowering parterres. Here, among the dazzling gilded bronze statues and foaming water jets, we witness the Great Cascade descending wide marble steps, the Fountain of Samson – where Samson battles with a lion that has a high water jet rising from its jaws – and a 300 metre canal extending into the sea.

On the sides of the canal, immersed in green boskets scored by a network of straight avenues traced with a pitchfork, we find other fountains and elegant pavilions, the names of which – Monplaisir, Marly, Ermitage – betray Peter the Great's admiration of France.

Opposite, above: The Upper Gardens, which look out over the south wing of the Great Palace. The gardens are arranged around a long central axis flanked by trimmed linden trees and avenues, and feature pergolas, symmetrically positioned beds of grass, statues and fountains – including that of Neptune, god of the seas, surrounded by nymphs, puttos, dolphins and dragons. Opposite, bottom: The fountain of Triton. Above: The Upper Gardens, covered in snow.

Where:
2 Razvodnaya Road, as you enter St Petersburg.

Getting there: By hydrofoil from the pier in front of the Hermitage Museum, or by train from the Baltiysky Station to Novy Peterhof, and then by bus no. 350, 351, 352 or 356.

Visiting hours: From May to the middle of October, it is open every day except Monday, and the last Tuesday of the month, from 10:00 to 18:00; the fountains function from 11:00 to 17:00. During the rest of the year, you can only visit the Great Palace, every day except Monday and the last Tuesday of the month, from 11:00 to 18:00.

Information: tel. 007 812 4277425; fax. 007 812 4279330; peterhofmuseum@mail.ru

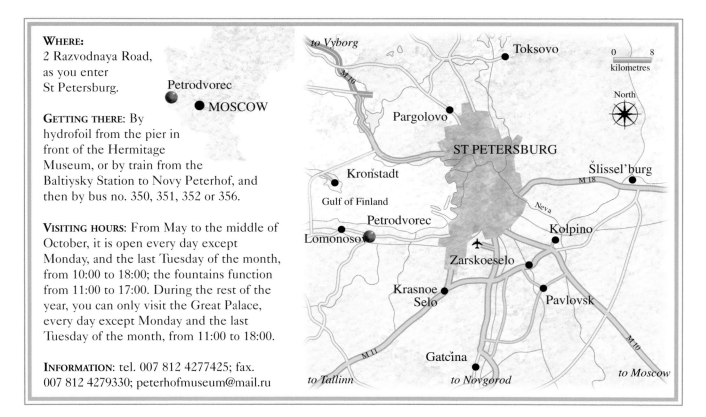

The Garden of Love (Villandry, France)

76

VAUX-LE-VICOMTE *The first example of a garden in the French style, beautiful enough to make the Sun King envious.*

The feast to celebrate the inauguration of the chateau of Vaux-le-Vicomte, on 17 April 1661, was a memorable event. Among the thousands of invitees was Louis XIV, curious to see the new residence of his Finance Minister, the mighty Nicolas Fouquet. The guests strolled at length in the park designed by André Le Nôtre, a rising star in the world of landscape gardeners, admiring the gentle slope of the area, which was larger than anything they had ever seen, rich in surprises and arranged with a geometrical rigour that celebrated the submission of Nature to the principle of Reason. All praised the lengthy perspectives capturing a sense of the infinite; the central avenue flanked by a double row of water jets, which looked like a wonderful crystal balustrade; the majestic transversal canal, deliberately hidden in a hollow to inspire awe when visitors suddenly came across it; and then the wide, square stretch of water in which the palace façade is reflected – a deliberate optical illusion makes the reflection appear at the foot of an enormous water lily. The guests also praised the three types of parterres created by Le Nôtre on the sides of the central avenue: the elegant *parterres de broderie*, with spirals of boxwood as subtle as filigree winding between the statues; the more subtle English-style parterres, with impeccable expanses of lawn enhanced by two circular water basins, and above all the colourful *parterres de piéces coupées pour les fleurs*, which, instead of being banished to the side of the house, had acquired a prestigious position next to the greatest *parterre de broderie*, displaying flowerbeds filled with the brightest flowers.

PARTERRES: EMBROIDERED FLOWERBEDS

Parterres – level spaces without trees and decorated like carpets – were created by Italian gardeners of the sixteenth century. To enhance the terraces closest to the palace, and to soften the architectural transition between the house and the garden, they had started to use low borders of boxwood or myrtle in addition to statues and fountains: perfectly trimmed humpbacked hedgerows that traced initials, coats of arms or geometric figures. These flowerbeds, often decorated with sculpted shrubs according to the art of topiary, were not created for walking but for the pleasure of the views they offered, and their layout could best be appreciated from the first floor windows of the palace. The spaces among the hedgerows were filled with sand or gravel – ephemeral flowers were not permitted, because the object was to create a Renaissance garden with an unchanging appearance, which only evergreen plants could guarantee. Enhanced and renovated, parterres also characterized the French gardens of the seventeenth century. Here the super-subtle boxwood hedgerows were used as 'embroidery thread' to trace complex arabesques, vine-branches, curves and spirals that broke off on a coloured background created with iron filings, clay or charcoal dust, marble or slate gravel and flowers. These were planted close together and chosen for their colour in order to form uniform surfaces of the same height.

RIGHT: *THE CROWN BASIN, WHICH YOU FIND ON YOUR LEFT AS YOU LEAVE THE CASTLE.*
ABOVE: *ONE OF THE TWO STATUES THAT DECORATE THE PARTERRE DE BRODERIE (OPPOSITE, TOP, DETAIL) WHICH ONE CAN ADMIRE WALKING ALONG THE LONG CENTRAL AXIS OF THE GARDEN.*
OPPOSITE: *ANOTHER GLIMPSE OF THE CASTLE AND OF THE GRASS PARTERRES ('ENGLISH' PARTERRES) EXTENDING ON THE RIGHT.*

ABOVE AND LEFT: *THE* PARTERRE
DE BRODERIE *WITH BOXWOOD*
HEDGEROWS THAT EMBROIDER THE
RED CLAY DUST. ALONG THE BORDERS
ARE YEWS IN THE SHAPES OF CONES
AND SPHERES. IN THE BACKGROUND,
YOU CAN GLIMPSE A GROTTO WITH
NUMEROUS SCULPTURES AND A LAWN
THAT FEATURES A STATUE OF
HERCULES.

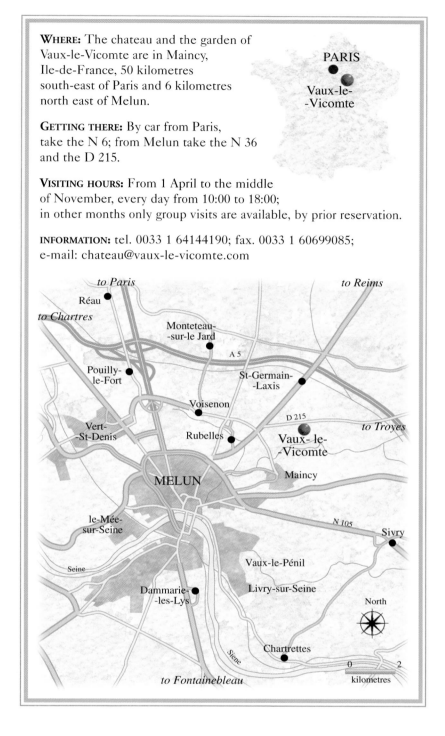

WHERE: The chateau and the garden of Vaux-le-Vicomte are in Maincy, Ile-de-France, 50 kilometres south-east of Paris and 6 kilometres north east of Melun.

GETTING THERE: By car from Paris, take the N 6; from Melun take the N 36 and the D 215.

VISITING HOURS: From 1 April to the middle of November, every day from 10:00 to 18:00; in other months only group visits are available, by prior reservation.

INFORMATION: tel. 0033 1 64144190; fax. 0033 1 60699085; e-mail: chateau@vaux-le-vicomte.com

Against the backdrop of the scenic *grille d'eau*, a comedy written specially by Molière unfolded. Then, towards evening, the tired guests retreated to the palace, where, to the sound of music composed by Lully, they were refreshed at a sumptuous banquet served on plates of gold. The surprises were not over, however, because Catherine wheels began to explode from the back of a gigantic whale that had appeared on the canal. At this point, the King decided he had had enough and abandoned the lively party in a foul mood. The great garden and the wonderful feast had angered him, convincing him that the rumours (spread by Fouquet's political enemies) were true: to allow himself such wild luxuries, his Minister of Finance had surely drawn from State coffers. And so, shortly after the inauspicious feast, Fouquet was arrested by a musketeer named D'Artagnan, ending his life in prison while his residence was confiscated and stripped of its most precious fittings.

Without the statues, fountains, vases and even trees, that were eradicated and transported to Versailles by Order of the King, the Park of Vaux began a long, unhappy period, ending only towards the beginning of the twentieth century when the work of Elie Lainé and Achille Duchêne, which departed a little from the original model, restored this perfect example of a classic, French garden to its earlier splendour.

VERSAILLES *A masterpiece in the formal, French style – the true symbol of the power of Louis XIV.*

After taking the reins of power in France, Louis XIV decided to build a palace of unprecedented proportions as a symbol of his ambitious political project: to reorganise the State, subordinating each local power to the central authority of the Sovereign.

The new residence, where the King repaired with his court in order to keep an eye on the more difficult members of the nobility, had to be extraordinary and prestigious: a model to admire and perhaps to imitate, but certainly not anything common mortals could ever hope to equal.

The area chosen for this demanding project was Versailles, a modest village at the gates of Paris, linked to happy childhood memories and where the King's father, Louis XIII, owned a small hunting chateau. The conditions of the area were decidedly unfavourable: the hill was too small to permit an enlargement of the chateau, and moreover the grounds were marshy and lacking in the water supplies required to feed the great number of fountains, canals and stretches of water that the park would have to accommodate. Instead of reconsidering, the King decided to experience 'the superb pleasure of taming nature' affirmed by Louis Saint-Simon.

The works began in 1661 and lasted more than fifty years, consisting of continual enlargements, developing under the direct control of the King and requiring huge resources. These included hundreds of horses and thousands of men, who were often forced to work under the hardest conditions. For example, to make the gardens suddenly 'appear in all their glory', the men had to eradicate, transport and plant enormous trees from forests in the middle of France. Massive displacements of earth permitted the men to enlarge the hill destined to receive the new palace, while

A GUIDED TOUR FROM A KING

The gardens played an important role in receiving guests and walks in the park were a necessary habit for the court and its guests. Much loved by the Sun King, who was fairly fit, these walks presented something of a problem for many of the nobility in his train, who were little inclined to physical activity. As one lady of the court wrote in her diary, 'here people hobble along like geese. Apart from the King, I don't know anyone who can walk just a few yards without puffing and panting'. For this reason, special litters carried by servants were arranged for ladies in particular.

But in any case, one could not walk freely or casually across the gardens. The visits were carefully choreographed, avoiding less scenic routes and choosing routes according to the rank of the guest. This assessment was made by the King, who wrote a guide outlining twelve different itineraries. These were always planned in advance to allow an army of gardeners, working until daybreak, to attend to every detail: raking the sand of the avenues, carrying rare plants to the boskets along the intended route and replacing flowers that were only slightly spoiled in the parterres. The fountain attendants had to remain on the alert, whistling to set in motion water for the jets lining the route of the royal procession.

LEFT: *LOUIS XIV IN A SCULPTURE BY GIAN LORENZO BERNINI. TOP: DETAIL OF THE ENTRANCE GATE. OPPOSITE: STRETCHES OF WATER IN FRONT OF THE CENTRAL BODY OF THE PALACE ARE DECORATED WITH BRONZE STATUES REPRESENTING THE MAIN FRENCH RIVERS (IN THE FOREGROUND, THE RHONE RIVER).*

another hill was completely levelled to make room for the great canal – conceived, like the whole garden, by André Le Nôtre. Drainage works to reclaim the grounds also got underway and, to feed the hydraulic system, the course of a river was first deviated, and then enormous and expensive installations at Marly channelled water from the Seine.

The layout of the garden is not very different from that of Vaux-le-Vicomte: a very long central axis equipped with a series of parterres, boskets and water basins. But for Versailles, Le Nôtre envisaged a network of avenues crossing each other at right angles or radiating outwards like stars, multiplying the infinite perspectives, to suggest the idea of a garden that had conquered the entire landscape.

From the terrace built in front of the central body of the palace, decorated by two immense stretches of water, and flanked by English-style *parterres de broderie*, one can still admire the path arrangements along the three-kilometre central axis. First is the Latona Basin, followed by a grassy carpet on the gentle slope of the King's Avenue leading to the Apollo Fountain, and then the brilliant basin of the Grand Canal, an immense surface measuring 23 hectares, where mock naval battles were organised for the famous feasts of Versailles.

Along the two avenues arranged parallel to the principal avenue, twelve boskets were laid out, planted with trees of

ABOVE: *THE LATONA BASIN, ARRANGED ALONG THE CENTRAL AXIS OF THE GARDEN AND REPRESENTING A SCENE FROM OVID'S* METAMORPHOSES. *THE CENTRAL CHARACTER IS LATONA (FAR RIGHT), MOTHER OF APOLLO AND OF DIANA. BEYOND THIS BASIN IS THE KING'S AVENUE, A WIDE GRASSY CARPET ON A GENTLE SLOPE, AND THE APOLLO FOUNTAIN (OPPOSITE, BOTTOM). THE GROUP OF SCULPTURES BY JEAN-BAPTISTE TUBY REPRESENT THE SUN GOD DRIVING HIS CHARIOT AND BRINGING LIGHT TO A NEW DAY. BEYOND THE FOUNTAIN BEGINS THE GRAND CANAL, A GLEAMING WATER BASIN IN THE SHAPE OF A CROSS, WITH ARMS MEASURING 1,800 AND 1,500 METRES. OPPOSITE, TOP: APOLLO BATHING. RIGHT: ONE OF THE FOUNTAINS REPRESENTING THE SEASONS, AT THE FOUR KEY POINTS OF THE BOSKETS ON THE SIDES OF THE CENTRAL AXIS: BACCHUS AMONG BUNCHES OF GRAPES AND SATYRS, SYMBOLISING AUTUMN.*

medium height and enclosed by yew and hornbeam hedgerows concealing fabulous surprises. For example, a 'water theatre' with 200 jets of seven height variations, or a ballroom in the shape of an amphitheatre with steps covered in grass, or a labyrinth enhanced by fountains that represented scenes from Aesop's fables. The most admired bosket was that created by the architect, Hardouin Mansart: a circular space enclosed by alternating marble columns and small water basins, embellished at the centre by a sculpture by François Girardon, the *Rape of Persephone*.

The gardens were decorated with thousands of marble and bronze vases, a great quantity inspired by the myth of Apollo, the God of the Sun, that Louis XIV had assumed as an emblem. In the park there were also woods and game preserves, an orangery where more than 3,000 plants in vases were covered in winter, a seraglio that hosted precious collections of exotic animals, and a private garden, the Grand Trianon, where the Sun King could give full rein to his passion for flowers, and where his rarest plants grew, including several orange trees cultivated in the earth under small glasshouses.

Here at times the King would order the gardeners to completely redo the flowerbeds while, with more intimate friends, he lunched in the elegant pavilion created by Mansart. With unparalleled splendours, and miles of tree-lined avenues that extended as far as the eye could see, the immense gardens of the Palace of Versailles were a clear metaphor for the absolute rule of the Sun King over the entire nation, a political declaration for the entire world in fact. But they are also a dazzling example of the formal French style, a masterpiece in which the great André Le Nôtre showed his skill in reconciling sumptuous and delicate tastes and wielding immense proportions harmoniously.

ABOVE: *THE ORANGERY, FLANKED BY STATELY STEPS, LOOKS OUT OVER THE ENORMOUS, ARTIFICIAL SWISS LAKE, NAMED IN HONOUR OF THE SWISS GUARDS WHO BUILT IT IN 1678. OPPOSITE: THE PARTERRE THAT YOU CAN SEE FROM THE GRAND TRIANON, WITH BOXWOOD HEDGEROWS AND BRIGHT BLOOMS. THE GRAND TRIANON WAS THE PRIVATE RESIDENCE OF THE SUN KING WHERE HE COULD REST, FAR FROM THE CHAOS OF THE COURT. ONE OF THE KING'S PASSIONS WAS FLOWERS AND THE FLOWERBEDS INCLUDED A SEEMINGLY INFINITE NUMBER OF LILIES, TULIPS, CARNATIONS, NARCISSUSES…*

WHERE: The gardens and chateau are in the centre of Versailles, 22 kilometres from Paris.

GETTING THERE: By train from Paris, take the RER C line to Versailles-rive-gauche-chateau; from Montparnasse station, the SNCF train to Versailles-Chantiers; from Saint-Lazare station, the SNCF train to Versailles-rive-droite; by bus from Pont de Sèvres, bus 171 to Versailles-Place d'Armes; by car, the A 13 motorway A 13 (toward Rouen), taking the Versailles-Château exit.

VISITING HOURS: The park is open every day from 7:00 in the summer and from 8:00 in the winter, until sunset. To explore the more remote areas of the park, bicycles and carriages are available.

INFORMATION: tel. 0033 1 30847400; e-mail: service.multimedia@chateauversailles.fr

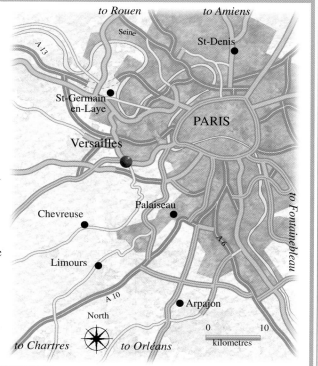

GIVERNY *Among water lilies and roses, lights and transparencies, is the garden that inspired Claude Monet.*

In the spring of 1882, the painter Claude Monet and his family moved to Giverny, a small village in the heart of Normandy. About a hectare of land between the road and the big pink house with green shutters was occupied by a typical *clos normand*, an orchard protected by stone walls and divided in two by an avenue lined with pines, yews and boxwood hedgerows. The master of impressionism did not like these plants and was eager to cut them down. Only the two yew trees closest to the house were saved at the request of his wife, Alice.

Monet's idea was to create a garden to paint – rich in flowers, colours, lights and transparencies, with plants selected and combined on the basis of their chromatic value and then left to grow freely, to imitate the exuberance of nature as much as possible. For this reason many fruit trees were sacrificed and in their place, on the big lawn strewn with daisies, poppies and cornflowers, a large group of ornamental *prunus*, apple and cherry trees appeared, much loved by the Master for their spring blooms.

To reproduce the bright colours of the blankets of hyacinths, tulips and narcissuses that Monet had admired during a stay in Holland, he designed several long, narrow, rectangular flowerbeds with thick plantations of irises, tulips, gladioli, anemones, corn poppies, asters and dahlias. With their spectacular blooms, they could create a bright play of colours that changed with the seasons.

Along the borders of the central avenue, covered with a series of metallic green arches carrying clematises and climbing roses, he planted more roses mixed with delphiniums, peonies, sunflowers and lilies, as well as a colourful carpet of nasturtiums that appeared at the start of summer.

In 1893, ten years after his arrival at Giverny, Monet bought another piece of ground, of around 8,000 square metres, immediately

LEFT: *THE PAINTER, CLAUDE MONET (1840–1926), WAS ALSO A LEARNED BOTANIST AND ENTHUSIASTIC GARDENER.* ABOVE: *THE FAMOUS POND WITH WATER LILIES IN THE GARDEN OF GIVERNY, WHICH MONET PERSONALLY CREATED AND TENDED FROM 1883. THE WATER LILIES WERE ONE OF HIS FAVOURITE SUBJECTS (*TOP: *ONE OF THE 200 PAINTINGS DEDICATED TO THESE FLOWERS). AFTER YEARS OF NEGLECT FOLLOWING THE DEATH OF THE PAINTER, THE GARDEN WAS RESTORED BETWEEN 1977 AND 1980, USING FLOWERS (IRISES, ROSES, EASTERN POPPIES, PEONIES, DAISIES, CORNFLOWERS, DAHLIAS, ETC.) THAT WERE AS CLOSE AS POSSIBLE TO THOSE CHOSEN BY MONET (*OPPOSITE*).*

LEFT AND BELOW: *LIGHTS AND COLOURS WERE COMBINED ACCORDING TO THE IMPRESSIONISTIC PALETTE. THE RESTORATION FAITHFULLY RECONSTRUCTED THE LAYOUT OF PLANTS AND TRIED ALSO TO RECREATE THE ATMOSPHERE OF THE WHOLE.*

OPPOSITE: *ANOTHER FAVOURITE SUBJECT OF CLAUDE MONET WAS THE JAPANESE BRIDGE, REFLECTED TOGETHER WITH POPLARS AND WEEPING WILLOWS IN THE WATERS OF THE LILY POND. ON ITS BANKS, MONET PLANTED TWO WISTERIAS, ONE WHITE AND ONE LILAC, WHICH YOU CAN STILL FIND IN THE GARDEN TODAY.*

above the railway line that marked the confines of his *clos normand*. Here, taking advantage of the presence of a stream and winning over the anxieties of his neighbours, who were afraid that this whimsical painter might pollute the water with his strange plants, the beautiful flowery lake immortalised in the canvases of the great master took form.

An exotic and secret corner of the garden, inspired by the Japanese gardeners that Monet had admired in a series of stamps he had collected, developed around a pool of water covered with water lilies, and surrounded by a vegetation thick with poplars, willows, bamboos, azaleas, irises, agapanthuses and rhododendrons.

A local artisan had also built a green wooden bridge copied from a Japanese print: framed by white wisteria and mallow, it completed a water garden rich in transparencies, filtered lights and reflected images – a sort of upside-down world transformed by the liquid element – and inspired the famous series of paintings, *Water Lilies*, of which almost 200 are preserved in the Paris Orangery Museum.

With the passing of the years, Monet had become a great botany enthusiast. Reading gardening books and magazines avidly, he had started an earnest exchange of plants and bulbs with his friends Clémenceau and Caillebotte. He was always on the lookout for rare varieties of plants, which he ordered regardless of the cost from nurserymen of the calibre of Vilmorin and, for water lilies, from Latour-Marliac: 'I'm spending all my money on the garden', he often confessed to friends. Preferring simple plants and flowers, he loved to mix the more humble flowers like primroses, daisies and forget-me-nots with the more sophisticated species.

Monet was proud of his garden, in which he strolled many times a day, whatever the season, and even more proud of his pond, conceived and moulded as a testing ground for a painting *en plein air*, which had to capture the mutability of nature and the even more complex mobility of light. He was happy to show the garden to friends and acquaintances as long as they arrived before five in the evening, the hour in which the flowers began to close.

When Monet became ill in 1926, the garden was lovingly tended by his daughter-in-law, Blanche. On his death, however, a period of

ABOVE: THE HOUSE WHERE CLAUDE MONET LIVED UNTIL HIS DEATH IN 1926. ROSES COVER THE FAÇADE, INCLUDING THE SAME 'MERMAID' THAT THE PAINTER PLANTED AND THAT WAS AMONG HIS FAVOURITES FOR ITS SIMPLE COROLLA. YOU REACH THE HOUSE AFTER WALKING DOWN AN AVENUE OF GREEN METALLIC ARCHES COVERED WITH ROSES (RIGHT). RIGHT, TOP: MORE ROSES ALONG A PATH BORDERED WITH STRIPS OF LAWN.

92

neglect began, ending only in 1977 when the *Académie des Beaux Arts*, the new proprietors of Giverny, began the work of restoration.

Recreating the splendours of Monet's time was not easy, given that so little remained of the house and garden. The windowpanes were in pieces after bombings, the wainscoting had decayed, the staircase had collapsed and the master's big studio had been invaded by weeds. With patience, varieties of plants similar to those chosen by Monet were tracked down, the lake was rebuilt and the famous Japanese bridge, which by now was too ruined to salvage, was reconstructed. The white and lilac wisteria that cover it remain those that the master planted.

Finally, in 1980, the garden that inspired Monet for more than twenty years, and which had hosted figures like Zola, Cézanne, Proust and Pissarro, regained its original appearance and was opened to the public.

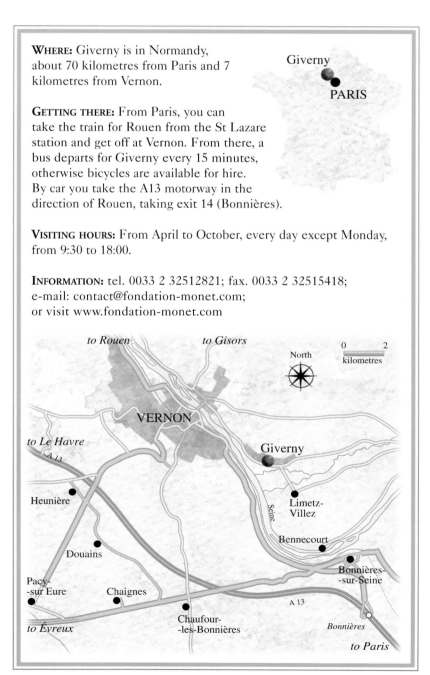

WHERE: Giverny is in Normandy, about 70 kilometres from Paris and 7 kilometres from Vernon.

GETTING THERE: From Paris, you can take the train for Rouen from the St Lazare station and get off at Vernon. From there, a bus departs for Giverny every 15 minutes, otherwise bicycles are available for hire. By car you take the A13 motorway in the direction of Rouen, taking exit 14 (Bonnières).

VISITING HOURS: From April to October, every day except Monday, from 9:30 to 18:00.

INFORMATION: tel. 0033 2 32512821; fax. 0033 2 32515418; e-mail: contact@fondation-monet.com; or visit www.fondation-monet.com

VILLANDRY *The most imaginative revival of the French Renaissance garden, featuring cabbages, pumpkins and artichokes.*

You cannot see the Gardens of Villandry, hidden as they are by the imposing outline of the castle, unless you look out of the window of the high terrace that runs along the eastern side. Nestled beside a thickly wooded hill, the orchards and the village with its grey, stern, pitch-roofed houses reveal themselves in all their beauty. The terrace structure, the perfect symmetry and the composition of the plants, immediately make one think of the French Renaissance style. Even experts, at first glance, find it hard to believe that these gardens are in fact less than one hundred years old – the fruit of a bold, single-minded restoration initiated in the 1920s by a Spaniard in love with the sixteenth century.

Even if little documented, the castle of Villandry has an ancient history. It was in built in 1532 for Jean le Breton, who was first an ambassador in Italy, and then Minister of Finance for Francis I. Le Breton razed a pre-existing fortress from the twelfth century to the ground – only the foundation and donjon remain. Little is known about what happened at Villandry in the centuries that followed, except that in 1754 it became the property of a certain Marquis de Castellane and that, in the nineteenth century, the original formal garden was destroyed to make room for an English-style park in fashion at the time. This is what it was in 1906, when it was bought by Joachim Carvallo, the great-grandfather of the present owner, and his wife Ann Coleman.

THE CASTLE OF VILLANDRY IS FAMOUS FOR ITS ORNAMENTAL AND KITCHEN GARDENS (RIGHT AND OPPOSITE, BOTTOM), COMPOSED OF A SERIES OF SQUARES (NINE IN ALL), EACH IN TURN SUBDIVIDED INTO BEDS WITH GEOMETRIC DESIGNS CREATED BY COMBINING DIFFERENT VEGETABLES AND FLOWERS. HERE AND THERE, IN THE CORNERS OF THE SQUARES, ROMANTIC GAZEBOS OFFER AN OPPORTUNITY TO REST. VILLANDRY ALSO OFFERS A SPLENDID EXAMPLE OF TOPIARY ART IN THE GARDEN OF LOVE (OPPOSITE, TOP) ON THE WEST SIDE OF THE CASTLE. TOP: RED ORNAMENTAL CABBAGES.

AROUND FORTY SPECIES OF VEGETABLES ARE GROWN IN THE KITCHEN GARDEN, ARRANGED IN BEDS ACCORDING TO THE SEASON: PEAS, BROAD BEANS, LETTUCES, TOMATOES, CABBAGES (LEFT: THE 'FRANKI' VARIETY WITH A WHITE CORE), RED-RIBBED ORNAMENTAL SWISS CHARD, SILVER-LEAFED ARTICHOKES, AND FINALLY THE SQUASHES, TRUE WINTER QUEENS AND SYMBOLS OF ABUNDANCE AND FERTILITY (OPPOSITE). ALL THESE VEGETABLES ARE DIVIDED AMONG THE OWNERS OF THE CASTLE, THE CARVALLO FAMILY, AND THE GARDENERS, BUT IF THE HARVEST IS ABUNDANT THEY ARE OFFERED TO VISITORS.

FLOWERS AND VEGETABLES: AN OLD ALLIANCE

The Romans, who were excellent gardeners, were the first to practise mixed cultures, creating small enclosed gardens in which they grew fruit trees, vegetables and flowers together. But it was in the Medieval period that this practice of mixing ornamental and vegetable plants attained its highest form. Hortus conclusus *was born in the privacy of monasteries – a space enclosed by high walls, with a fountain at the centre, subdivided in themes: beds dedicated to medicinal plants (*verziere*), those with fruit trees and vegetables (*pomario*) those with perennial, arboreal species (*viridario*) and finally those reserved for flowers. These last had a symbolic significance: the rose was an emblem of the Madonna, lilies alluded to purity and violets to modesty.*

From the fifteenth century, ornamental and kitchen gardens took different paths: the first, modelled according to principles relating to geometry, proportion and symmetry, became the stage of the owner's public life, a place to display social status; the second allowed the owner to retreat into a more domestic, private dimension. Yet even here, in what is often a small, but precious scrap of ground that sustains the family, there is still a corner reserved for flowers: cosmos, dahlias, gladioli, asters, etc. Nothing to compare with the triumphant jardin potager *of Villandry perhaps, yet the pleasure of combining the practical with the pleasurable is undeniable.*

Inspired by the drawings that illustrated *Les plus excellents bastiments de France* by Jacques Androuet du Cerceau (1576–79), Carvallo decided to restore the garden to a rudimentary Renaissance structure: an ambitious and difficult undertaking which the Spaniard set about inspired by a romantic but nostalgic vision of the past. He was convinced of the necessity to foil 'social progress', by which, in his words, 'men and their property were sliding imperceptibly towards the stables, while animals were able to enter the lounge with the minimum of difficulty'.

The restoration works dragged on until 1918, when the gardens assumed the appearance they retain up to this day. Arranged on three levels, the highest holds the Water Garden, a vast liquid mirror, hidden by a curtain of yews and inhabited by swans and wild geese, which is not only ornamental, but irrigates and feeds the fountains. At the level below, you find an ornamental garden, where several symbolic themes are illustrated in extremely refined detail. There is the Garden of Love, in which the boxwood figures accompanied by coloured flowers symbolise the different characters of amorous passion: fickle love (butterfly wings and fans), tender love (hearts and masks), tragic love (dagger blades) and passionate love (shattered hearts). In spring white and pink tulips, violas, pansies, daisies and forget-me-nots spill over the boxwood hedgerows, replaced in summer by sage, begonias, verbenas and red and yellow dahlias.

LEFT: *IN THE GARDEN OF LOVE, ON THE SOUTH SIDE OF THE CASTLE* (OPPOSITE), *LOW BOXWOOD HEDGEROWS OUTLINE HEARTS AND MASKS, SYMBOLS OF TENDER LOVE; SHATTERED HEARTS, SYMBOLS OF PASSIONATE LOVE; AND FANS AND BUTTERFLY WINGS, SYMBOLS OF FICKLE LOVE. BELOW: YEW TREES AMONG THE HEDGEROWS.*

WHERE: In the district of Indre-et-Loire, about 250 kilometres from Paris and 15 kilometres from Tours.

GETTING THERE: From Paris by car, take the Tours exit from the A10 and travel 15 kilometres along the D7; from Paris by train, take the TGV, Paris Montparnasse to Tours; by bus from the Tours station, take the Villandry Tour shuttle.

VISITING HOURS: The gardens are open the whole year round, every day from 9:00 in the morning until sunset. Guided tours are available.

INFORMATION: Château de Villandry, 37510 Villandry; tel. 0033 (2) 47500209; fax. 0033 (2) 47501285; e-mail: info@chateauvillandry.com

Nearby, we find the Garden of Music, where the boxwood and yew hedgerows trace harps, lyres and musical notes. On the other side of the canal we find the Herb Garden, cosy and intimate, protected by a pergola of antique vines, and hosting 32 species of aromatic plants, which include fennel and angelica, absinthe and sage, myrtle and field balm, melissa and camomile. The classic hornbeam labyrinth is not absent either – recently restored, a panoramic turret rises from its centre.

On the lowest terrace, next to the Herb Garden, extends the true jewel of Villandry: the *jardin potager*, or Kitchen Garden. Laid out over a surface of 12,500 square metres, and subdivided into nine squares separated by little paths, each square is defined by a low treillage of oak splints decorated by old apple trees, cut into cords and pruned into spindle shapes, resulting in a design that combines vegetables of different form and colour so that the Kitchen Garden looks like a coloured chessboard from above.

From March to June the beds are dominated by lettuces, peas, broad beans, lentils, tomatoes, peppers, cabbages, Swiss chard and red and yellow squashes. There are about forty different species, 90,000 vegetables per year and over 30,000 flowering plants decorate the borders.

This fabulous Kitchen Garden was not only intended to display its beauty but to be productive: the harvest is shared among the owner's family and the gardeners. In periods of abundance it is offered to visitors, while the spoiled vegetables are fed to the compost heap. Only natural fertilizers are used and weeds are pulled out by hand instead of using weed killers. In addition, crops are rotated so as not to tire the soil – an example of sound ecological administration.

CHATSWORTH
PARK
(ENGLAND)

100

CHATSWORTH *A masterful synthesis of* *landscape styles and one of the most famous gardens in England.*

The park of Chatsworth House, the sumptuous residence of the Dukes of Devonshire, exhibits landscape styles and fashions that span a period of four centuries. The construction of this august mansion and garden began quietly in the sixteenth century and was resumed with vigour at the end of the seventeenth century, after its baronet owners became counts and dukes. Desiring to conform to the French style which ruled the day, the owners had engaged two famous landscape artists – Henry Wise and George London – who transformed the slopes immediately around the house into a series of terraces containing *parterres de broderie*, boxwood figures sculpted according to the rules of topiary, boskets and geometrically shaped stretches of water. Miles of hedgerows were planted and long avenues flanked by trees with a square trim were laid down. Among the marvels of the garden was a fountain, conceived for the amuse-

ment of the First Duke of Devonshire. Still working today, this gilded lead fountain in the shape of a willow tree would suddenly spurt water over unfortunate guests from its 'branches' and 'leaves'.

During this period, guests were struck by the uncomfortable contrast between the rigorous elegance of the garden and the wild, decidedly unattractive appearance of the surrounding countryside, which had been reduced to a gigantic swamp by the continuous flooding of the Derwent River. This discord was remedied towards the middle of the eighteenth century when the owners decided to remodel the extensive grounds. They turned to the young, but famous, Lancelot Brown, nicknamed 'Capability' because of his ability to identify potential in the most wretched areas.

Capability Brown decided to assign a leading role to the river. With the help of a small dyke and reinforcements for the banks, he

OPPOSITE: *THE WESTERN FAÇADE OF CHATSWORTH HOUSE. IN THE FOREGROUND, THE DERWENT RIVER AND PAINE'S BRIDGE (TOP: THE SAME BRIDGE SEEN FROM THE SOUTH-EAST). RIGHT: THE PRIVATE GARDEN THAT OCCUPIES THE TERRACE BESIDE THE HOUSE. FIRST CREATED IN 1820, IT WAS COMPLETELY RESTORED IN 1950. THE MOTIF CREATED WITH THE BOXWOOD HEDGEROWS AROUND THE TULIP FOUNTAIN IS DRAWN FROM A LAYOUT OF THE FAMOUS VILLA OF LORD BURLINGTON AT CHISWICK, IN TURN INSPIRED BY THE WORKS OF ANDREA PALLADIO.*

LEFT: *THE ORIGINAL WINDING BEECH HEDGEROWS, CREATED IN 1953 TO PROVIDE A FITTING FRAME FOR THE BUST OF WILLIAM SPENCER CAVENDISH, SIXTH DUKE OF DEVONSHIRE. WHEN THESE BEECHES WERE BEDDED, THEY WERE ONLY 45 CENTIMETRES HIGH. OPPOSITE: THE LABYRINTH, FORMED WITH IMMACULATE YEW HEDGEROWS. THIS WAS PLANTED IN 1962 IN PLACE OF THE GREAT STOVE, THE GREAT IRON GLASSHOUSE CREATED BY JOSEPH PAXTON IN THE NINETEENTH CENTURY AND DEMOLISHED IN 1920.*

transformed it into a presentable waterway, dignifying it with a Palladian bridge. Then he designed the immense park that still surrounds Chatsworth House today, creating, in accordance with the principles of the new landscape style, expansive, softly undulating lawns that eventually blended with groups of wisely positioned trees and the horizon.

Thus the once marshy grounds were transformed into a pleasant, apparently natural landscape, although in reality it had been planned with care and obtained only after titanic displacements of earth. This process erased a large part of the old formal garden, of which only the more attractive parts closest to the house were salvaged. One survivor was the Great Cascade, a scenic water staircase, conceived at the end of the seventeenth century by Grillet, a pupil of Le Nôtre. It has twenty-four steps of differing heights

created to obtain different sounds from the running water, and is enclosed at the highest point by an elegant pavilion in the form of a temple, created in 1711 by Thomas Archer.

Modifications continued during the nineteenth century, entrusted to the capable hands of Joseph Paxton, a brilliant gardener of Victorian England. Paxton enhanced Chatsworth House with a rock garden built from enormous stones stacked on top of one another to create a dramatic setting, and an arboretum in which 2,000 species of exotic trees were planted in record time.

Paxton also built the spectacular Emperor Fountain, equipped with a jet that was more than 90 metres high: a masterpiece of hydraulic engineering created for a visit, cancelled *in extremis*, from the Tsar of Russia. Paxton also indulged the sixth Duke of Devonshire's passion for

ABOVE: *The pavilion in the shape of a temple at the top of the Great Cascade, which consists of twenty-four steps of varying depth and height.* RIGHT: *The Broad Walk, an avenue 500 metres long, bordered first by trimmed yews and then by linden trees.* OPPOSITE, RIGHT: *The Valley of Rhododendrons;* LEFT: *The Conservative Wall, a complex of iron and wooden glasshouses that extend for more than 100 metres along a sharp incline. Designed by Paxton, these house figs, peaches, apricots and precious varieties of camellias.*

106

JOSEPH PAXTON, INNOVATOR

Joseph Paxton built the Crystal Palace in the heart of Hyde Park, in London, for the Great Exhibition of 1851. This boldly conceived building covered an area of 7 hectares, with gigantic glass panels supported by cast iron columns, and was equipped with an efficient ventilation system and protection against the sun to create a pleasant internal climate – nothing like the humid, suffocating environment of traditional glasshouses, from which annoyed visitors hastily beat a retreat.

Paxton achieved this significant result after experiments conducted at Chatsworth, where he had slowly developed more sophisticated glasshouses: from the Conservative Wall, a series of elegant constructions created for camellias, to the conservatory built in only three months to host the precious Victoria amazonica, *with a structure that imitated the complex nervation of the large leaves of this tropical water lily.*

The same principles were then adopted for the stately Great Stove, a 20-metre high glasshouse admired by Queen Victoria and Charles Darwin, which hosted not only a vast assortment of exotic plants, but tropical birds, silver- and gold-scaled fish swimming in basins of water and great crystalline rocks.

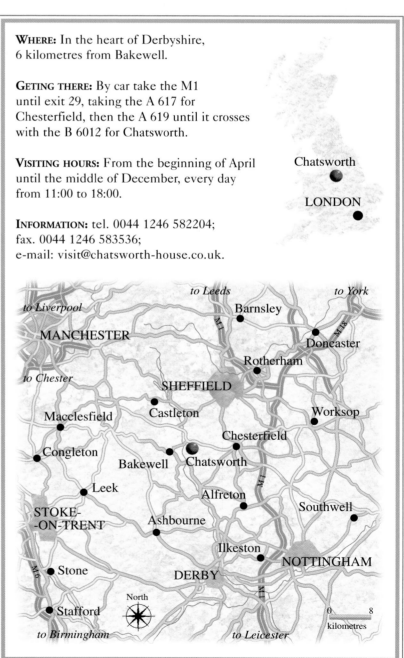

WHERE: In the heart of Derbyshire, 6 kilometres from Bakewell.

GETING THERE: By car take the M1 until exit 29, taking the A 617 for Chesterfield, then the A 619 until it crosses with the B 6012 for Chatsworth.

VISITING HOURS: From the beginning of April until the middle of December, every day from 11:00 to 18:00.

INFORMATION: tel. 0044 1246 582204; fax. 0044 1246 583536; e-mail: visit@chatsworth-house.co.uk.

botanical treasures with a series of innovative glasshouses, which permitted the successful cultivation of delicate, exotic plants. The most admired glasshouse was the enormous Great Stove, an iron and glass construction so large that Queen Victoria and Prince Albert used a carriage drawn by a span of horses to view it. The great glasshouse of Paxon was demolished in 1920. In its place today, one can admire a labyrinth that winds its way between impeccable walls of yews. Other more recent arrangements include the winding beech hedgerows planted in front of a circular stretch of water dating back to the seventeenth century, and the boxwood parterre on a terrace to the side of the house, which imitates a design from Lord Burlington's villa at Chiswick.

LEVENS HALL *Unchanged for more than 300 years and famous the world over for its original sculptures.*

This Elizabethan mansion, which, as tradition requires, is populated by all kinds of ghosts (including a small black dog that prowls around the entrance hall) also boasts the presence of a surreal assembly of plants trimmed into imaginative topiary shapes: gigantic boxwood and yew sculptures in the form of spirals and umbrellas, arches surmounted by crowns, and daring superimpositions of cones, cylinders, spheres and pyramids – these are the glories of the Levens Hall garden. They have miraculously preserved their late-seventeenth-century appearance, which was when they were planted by Colonel James Grahme, a gentleman who held the office of Privy Purse and Keeper of the Buckhounds in the court of King James II. After the forced abdication of the Sovereign in favour of his son-in-law, William of Orange, Grahme found himself unexpectedly out of work. He retired to Levens Hall, an estate that he had just purchased in the north of England, taking with him another victim of the change in government, the French designer-gardener, Monsieur Guillaume Beaumont, who had crossed the channel some time before to work on the royal gardens of Hampton Court.

At Levens Hall, Monsieur Beaumont was able to display his abilities by creating a formal garden that immediately earned him widespread admiration and made Colonel Grahme's garden popular with guests from all over England – visitors who didn't hesitate to tackle the long, uncomfortable journey along country roads to admire the straight avenues flanked by monumental beech hedgerows, the elegant geometric flowerbeds filled with flowers in the Dutch style then in fashion, and above all the fantastic shapes of the trimmed plants.

Perhaps it was just this unconditional appreciation that permitted

the green spaces of Levens Hall to escape the radical transformations imposed on all of Europe by the landscape style of the eighteenth century, which was relentless in wiping out any geometric garden design to make room for sinuous lanes, undulating grounds and free-growing plants.

The only attack to the formal layout of Levens Hall was launched at the end of the eighteenth century by Lady Andover, a distant predecessor of the current owner, who was in love with wild green spaces and who ordered her head gardener to leave off the pruning and to let ivy, honeysuckle and mignonette grow everywhere. This decision was promptly reversed by the granddaughter of this romantic lady, who fortunately managed to restore order to a garden that had begun to run wild.

And so today, exactly as it was three centuries ago, the topiary parterre still hosts around ninety boxwoods and yews, some three hundred years old. They are trimmed into a multitude of shapes invented by Monsieur Beaumont: the variety of figures and shapes give movement to the whole garden and offer a wide range of surprising views.

At the foot of this unusual forest of figures, crossed by straight avenues that intersect at right angles, is a thick carpet of flowers, not exactly those used in the times of Colonel Grahme, but still neatly arranged in geometric flowerbeds bordered by low boxwood hedgerows. The tidy plantations are renewed twice a year nowadays: in spring all types of violas, tulips and forget-me-nots, in summer dandelions, artemisias, helichrysums, heliotropes and verbenas.

In addition to the Topiary Garden, Levens Hall also offers other

ARCHES SURMOUNTED BY CROWNS (ABOVE), SPIRALS, SPHERES AND CYLINDERS STACKED ON TOP OF EACH OTHER (OPPOSITE, TOP), PYRAMIDS (LEFT) — THERE WERE NO LIMITS TO THE IMAGINATION OF GUILLAUME BEAUMONT WHEN HE PLANNED THE TOPIARY GARDEN OF LEVENS HALL. A FEW OF THE BOXWOODS AND YEWS THAT WE ADMIRE TODAY ARE THE VERY ONES THAT HE BEDDED AND MODELLED ACCORDING TO THE ART OF TOPIARY AT THE END OF THE SEVENTEENTH CENTURY. OPPOSITE: THE ENTRANCE TO THE HOUSE.

THE ANCIENT ART OF SCULPTING TREES

The Persians and Greeks practised topiary but, according to Pliny the Elder, the true inventor was the Roman cavalryman Gnaius Mattius, a contemporary of Emperor Augustus. Topiary is the art of trimming trees and shrubs to make them assume forms that are rigorously geometric or quite fantastic. The clever art of gardeners has transformed cypress, boxwood, holm oak, myrtle, rosemary etc. into prisms, pyramids, cones, human or animal figures and landscapes.

*After the fall of the Roman Empire, the art of topiary survived only in the small enclosed gardens of monasteries (*horti conclusi*), reduced to modest hedgerows of boxwood, santolina, or germander, which defined beds of medicinal and aromatic herbs. But from the fifteenth century, plant sculptures again became central features in gardens, in forms and styles that characterized individual countries: the Italian parterres were simple weavings created with aromatic herbs such as sweet marjoram, hyssop, rue and thyme, which enclosed violas, carnations and primroses; the sumptuous French* parterres de broderie *used miniature boxwood hedgerows as embroidery, to trace family emblems, enigmatic ciphers and arabesques; and the English knot gardens had as their main motif two hedgerows trimmed to look like a knot.*

It was England that precipitated the decline of topiary art. At the end of the eighteenth century, perhaps as a reaction to the extreme use of plant sculptures, the landscape garden established itself: a park more than a garden, with plants free to grow according to natural design. This was a style that would influence the whole of Europe. Many English topiary gardens were destroyed and Levens Hall is one of the few that has remained intact until today.

The bizarre forms of the topiary alternate with elegant, geometrically-shaped flowerbeds, consisting of boxwood hedgerows enclosing carpets of flowers. These flowers change with the seasons: tulips, violas and forget-me-nots in the spring; verbenas, artemisias and helychrisum in the summer.

WHERE: On the banks of Lake Windermere, Cumbria, about 8 kilometres south of Kendal, on the A6.

GETTING THERE: By car from Manchester, take the M6 (it takes about one and a half hours); by train go to Oxenholme station (which is about 8 kilometres from Levens Hall; there is a taxi rank right outside the station); by bus there is a service that runs from Grasmere, Ambleside, Windermere and Kendal, stopping outside Levens Hall once every hour.

VISITING HOURS: The gardens are open from the middle of April to the middle of October, every day except Friday and Saturday, from 10:00 to 17:00. You can visit the house between 12:00 and 17:00.

INFORMATION: Levens Hall, Kendal, Cumbria LA8 OPD; tel. 0044 (0)15395 60321; fax. 0044 (0)15395 60669; e-mail: email @levenshall.fsnet.co.uk

green jewels born of the creative abilities of Guillaume Beaumont, like the gigantic and compact beech hedgerows that flank the avenues at the back of the house. Other marvels were conceived in more recent periods, but they also emphasise the impeccable formal organization of the garden. For example, the parterre that follows a seventeenth-century design, with squares defined by boxwood borders, and hosting only plants that were used in English gardens three centuries ago, from primulas to the glorious white rose of York and the red rose of Lancaster. Or the Fountain Garden, with its circular water basin positioned at the intersection of two avenues, covered by a green tunnel formed by the interweaving branches of a double row of yews.

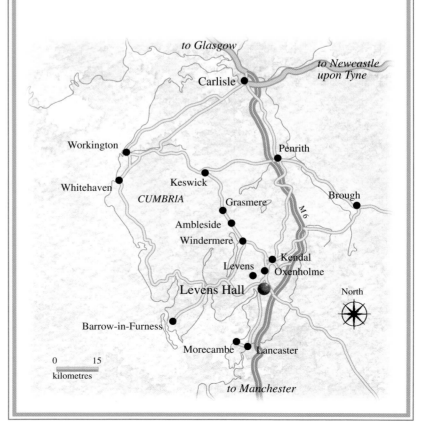

HIDCOTE MANOR *The first and most famous garden to contain a series of 'rooms', a surprising marriage of discipline and fantasy.*

Until 1907, Hidcote Manor was a small, wind-blown estate in Glouce-stershire without particular attraction. Then Lawrence Johnston, an American born in Paris, who before settling in Great Britain had lived in France, transformed it into the most famous and innovative English garden of the twentieth century. An exemplary model, it was esteemed by professionals like Russell Page and by amateurs across the world, who enthusiastically imitated its hedgerows that combined different species, its luxuriant borders of flowering plants and above all its very original 'rooms'. Here the principle of unity of composition, that for centuries had guided the design of gardens, was put aside to make room for a series of independent spaces, capable of satisfying a desire shared by many green enthusiasts: to host a variety of environments in one gar-den, without risking unpleasant contrasts.

Johnston – who could count not only on a huge inheritance, but on an undisputed talent for botany and a collaboration with Norah Lind-say, a talented and intuitive landscape artist – succeeded in creating and combining many gardens in one; a series of open-air 'rooms' differing in form, colour, dimension and design, surrounded by imposing hedge-rows that offered an excellent retreat from cold winds, and linked by green passages, grassy paths or expanses of lawn.

Each room was then 'furnished' with various plants and styles, alternating reason and emotion, intimacy and stateliness. In some, Johnston recreated the severe, formal atmosphere of classic gardens: simple lawns flanked by hornbeams with squared crowns to form an impeccable Italian-style palisade, or decorated with yews and boxwood trimmed according to the rules of topiary. In others, a strictly geome-trical background structure was sweetened by an irregular exuberance of plants arranged as in the natural gardens proposed by William Robinson: roses, flowering shrubs, herbaceous plants and bulbs mixed in an apparently spontaneous way, with garish climbers clambering merrily over the stern green walls of the hedgerows. In further rooms, Johnston designed lush borders mixed with herbaceous plants; against a background of yew hedgerows, these blend into one colour, or take up the multi-coloured schemes invented by Jekyll.

RIGHT: *The Long Walk, the grassy avenue that runs between hornbeam walls, cutting from north to south the network of 'rooms' that make up the garden. The gate at the bottom opens onto the countryside.* BELOW: *A resting point among the wisteria at the end of the Rose Walk.* OPPOSITE: *The border of peony and allium (top, detail) in the Pillar Garden. In the background, the thatched cottage that dominates the adjacent White Garden.*

ABOVE: *A PASSAGEWAY AMONG THE HORNBEAM WALLS.* RIGHT: *THE FUCHSIA GARDEN. IN THE FLOWERBEDS BORDERED BY LOW BOXWOOD HEDGEROWS, THE BLUE FLOWERS OF THE SPRING SQUILL GIVE WAY TO SUMMER FUCHSIAS. BEYOND THE SCULPTURES OF BIRDS IN YEW HEDGES, YOU CAN GLIMPSE THE CIRCLE, A ROOM OCCUPIED ENTIRELY BY A CIRCULAR FOUNTAIN.* OPPOSITE, TOP: *PEONY AND ALLIUM;* BELOW: *THE WATER BASIN COVERED IN WATER LILIES IN THE PINE GARDEN. ON THE SIDE, A FLOWERING CASCADE OF CEANOTHUS.*

The passage from one room to another holds many surprises. From the Fuchsia Garden, a stern parterre of fuchsias surrounded by a hedgerow combining hornbeam, yew, holly and beech, and offering a spectacular patchwork of textures and green shades, to a small space occupied almost entirely by a round water basin called The Circle.

Then the famous White Garden, ruled over by a thatched cottage, surrounded by high yew walls, rekindled in summer by the scarlet flowers of a climber and populated by doves sculpted in boxwood; the

MIXED BORDERS: THE ART OF PAINTING WITH FLOWERS

The mixed borders of herbaceous plants, one of the more characteristic elements of contemporary English gardens, are the invention of Gertrude Jekyll (1843-1932), painter and skilled landscape artist, who, at the end of the nineteenth century, applied an elaborate theory of Michel Eugène Chevreul, Director of Dyeworks at Gobelins, to the garden. This was based on complementary colours and the soft sequences of warm and cold colours. In her garden in Munstead Wood, Surrey, Jekyll had created a famous mixed border, which had to be viewed from a distance, like a painting, and where the plants had been combined according to a precise colour scheme: extremely cold colours to bring out the warmer ones in the centre.

One side began with blue, white and light-yellow flower bushes, moving towards increasingly stronger shades of yellow and finally to the orange and red zones. At the centre of the border, this sequence of colours was reversed, moving towards the cold colours: orange, fading yellows, white and pink, finishing with violet and lilac flowers surrounded by grey-leafed plants. The casual appearance of the mixed borders designed by Miss Jekyll concealed a profound expertise; the choice of plants was governed by a precise observation of every detail, down to the colour of the corollas at the time of flowering, which had to match those of the neighbouring flowers.

ABOVE: *THE WHITE GARDEN.
FROM SPRING TO AUTUMN THE
FLOWERBEDS OFFER A SUCCES-
SION OF WHITE FLOWERS
(TULIPS, ROSES, BELL FLOWERS)
OR GREY-SILVER LEAVES (SENE-
CO, CINERARIAS).* RIGHT: *THE
STATELY LEBANESE CEDAR THAT
TOWERS OVER THE OLD GARDEN.*
OPPOSITE, LEFT: *THE STILT
GARDEN* (OPPOSITE, RIGHT:
*FROM THE OTHER SIDE) WITH A
ROW OF HORNBEAMS: INTERWO-
VEN BRANCHES AND SQUARED
CROWNS FORM AN ITALIAN-STYLE
PALISADE. THE GATE AT THE
BOTTOM FRAMES A VIEW OF THE
COTSWOLDS.*

116

WHERE: In Gloucestershire, about 5 kilometres from Chipping Campden.

GETTING THERE: By car, take the A44 until the intersection with the B 4632 for Chipping Campden.

VISITING HOURS: The garden is open from the end of March to the beginning of November every day except Thursday and Friday, from 10:00 to 17:00.

INFORMATION: tel. 0044 1386 438333.

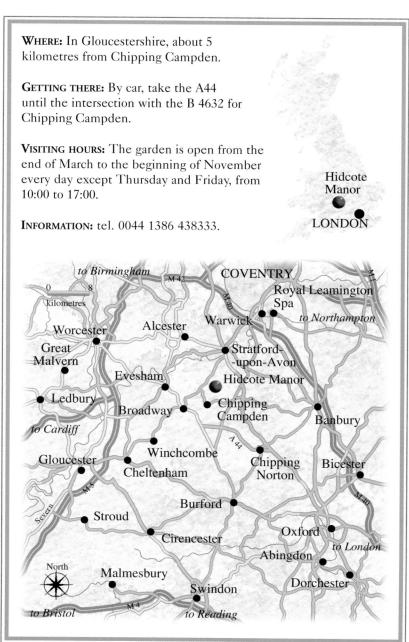

Pillar Garden, dominated by the solemn, austere outlines of gigantic yews trimmed into columns; the elegant green ellipse of the Theatre Lawn, shaded by a majestic beech; the rigour of a circular flowerbed of hellebore and lilac; and an expanse of *Hosta* and *Lysichiton* that open among magnolias, hydrangeas and *Osmanthus* in the Stream Garden.

In these 'rooms' Johnston gave free rein to his passion for exotic rarities that had driven him to participate in botanical expeditions – in South Africa with Cherry Ingram and in Yunnan with George Forrest – making room for species that had just arrived in Europe from China, Tibet and Japan: unusual varieties of camelias, rhododendrons, lilies, jasmine and Oregon grape. He also tested his abilities as a plantsman, inventing pairings that at the time were decidedly out of the ordinary, but that soon had a following. For example, the audacious red borders made up of tulips, sage, dahlias, roses and red verbenas, mixed with the purple leaves of *Heuchera* and *Berberis*; the more delicate pink and mauve borders obtained with bellflowers and hibiscus, iris and cinquefoil, peony and *Phlox*; and the combinations invented for the room dedicated to his mother, Mrs Windthrop: yellow day-lilies, acid-green *Euphorbia*, blue *Cynoglossum* and copper-coloured *Cordyline*.

HAMPTON COURT *Regal gardens for the residence of England's most famous sovereigns.*

When William III (William of Orange) ascended the throne of England in 1689, the violent asthma attacks that afflicted him determined the fortune of Hampton Court. The magnificent gardens of Het Loo had been built in Holland for William; now Hampton Court was chosen as the official residence of the sovereign for its position: close to London, but away from the polluted air of the capital. As soon as he arrived in England, William wasted no time in turning to the best landscape artists, to surround himself with greenery so that he would not regret what he had left behind.

The palace of Hampton Court, looking out from the banks of the Thames, was built in 1614 for Thomas Wolsey, Cardinal and Minister of Justice to Henry VIII, who also suffered from ill health. The area was chosen with care by a delegation of doctors who had combed the surroundings of London in search of a zone uncontaminated by the smoke and fumes of the capital. Unfortunately, Cardinal Wolsey was not able to breathe this clean air for long, because after his fall from grace, he was forced to relinquish Hampton Court to Henry VIII in 1525. The latter enhanced it with a series of delightful 'knot' gardens, the Renaissance predecessors of baroque parterres, and decorated it with rows of thyme and hyssop,

which crossed each other to form intricate designs.

In 1660, the residence fell into the hands of Charles II, who, having spent long periods in France, was keen to recreate at least some of the wonders he had witnessed beyond the Channel. So, on the east side of the palace, which housed the reception rooms, a monumental water canal was dug, which survives to this day. Almost a mile long, it was a sensational novelty for seventeenth-century England. It was a copy of the canal that his grandfather, Henry IV, had created at Fontainebleau, flanked on both sides by shady avenues with rows of yews that formed a wide semicircle at the foot of the palace. Perhaps it was also this, in addition to the clean air, that influenced William III to live at Hampton Court: it reminded him of his beloved Holland.

Thus the palace on the Thames was promoted from country residence to official residence: a transformation that entailed a demanding programme of works beginning in 1689, the day after the new sovereign's disembarkation in England. In the planning phase, William created an 'exhibition room' displaying the royal gardens created by George London, Henry Wise and above all, Daniel Marot, the designer of Het Loo.

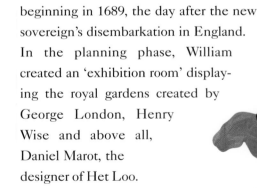

OPPOSITE, TOP: *THE WESTERN WING OF HAMPTON COURT PALACE: TURRETS, GABLES AND PICTURESQUE CHIMNEY POTS ARE A REMINDER OF THE TUDOR PERIOD, WHEN HENRY VII RULED (LEFT). IN CONTRAST, THE TYPICALLY BAROQUE SOUTH FAÇADE TAKES US BACK TO THE TIME OF WILLIAM OF ORANGE (RIGHT) WHO REIGNED BETWEEN 1689 AND 1702. IN FRONT OF THIS FAÇADE LIES THE RECENTLY RESTORED PRIVY GARDEN, ONCE THE PRIVATE GARDEN OF THE SOVEREIGN. CLOSED ON THE THAMES SIDE BY A WROUGHT IRON GATE, THE PRIVY GARDEN HAS AT ITS CENTRE A LARGE ROUND FOUNTAIN SURROUNDED BY ELEGANT GRASS PARTERRES, DECORATED BY YEWS, HOLLIES AND POTTED ORANGES.*

ABOVE AND OPPOSITE, TOP: *TWO OF THE LAKE GARDENS, SO CALLED BECAUSE AT ONE TIME, PERHAPS EVEN BEFORE THE REIGN OF HENRY VIII, THERE WERE FRESHWATER FISH TANKS FOR BREEDING FISH TO EAT IN THIS AREA OF THE GARDEN. TODAY IT HOSTS A FOUNTAIN AT THE CENTRE AND FLOWERBEDS.*

LEFT: *A GROUP OF PALMS. OPPOSITE, BOTTOM: THE FOUNTAIN GARDEN AND THE EASTERN FAÇADE OF THE PALACE. IN THE TIME OF WILLIAM III, THE GARDEN WAS EMBELLISHED WITH SIX LARGE FLOWERBEDS EMBROIDERED WITH BOXWOOD, THIRTEEN FOUNTAINS, AN IMMENSE NUMBER OF STATUES, AND YEWS AND HOLLIES TRIMMED INTO PYRAMID SHAPES.*

Marot transformed the arcade of yews into the sumptuous Fountain Garden, an immense area divided into six large flowerbeds. In the two closest to the palace he designed an elaborate *parterre de broderie* – boxwood spirals against a background of coloured gravel – while in the outer beds, Marot created a sober English parterre – carpets of lawn decorated with low boxwood hedges. To add distinction, he installed thirteen fountains (one of the king's passions), numerous statues and hundreds of yews and hollies trimmed into pyramid forms.

Of this entire design, only the central fountain remains, because Queen Anne, who succeeded William, could not stand the smell of boxwood, destroyed the parterre and substituted it with a simple lawn. Queen Anne eliminated the fountains and allowed the yews to grow, which today have reached a substantial height and have a curious 'mushroom' shape.

In front of the north façade of the palace, the royal gardeners then created a 'wilderness', a green space that, in spite of its name, had an absolutely formal layout, crossed by paths flanked by hornbeam hedges high enough to hide the view of the palace. Their interweaving branches formed a series of 'rooms', where benches and flowering shrubs were arranged. In the middle of the garden a high pine tree was planted and

Below and opposite, top: The Fountain Garden, at the point where it extends from the central fountain up to the wide canal created in the seventeenth century by Charles II. It was Queen Anne, who succeeded William III in 1702, who transformed the garden, eliminating parterres, substituting simple stretches of lawn, and leaving the yews, which today have a curious 'mushroom' shape, to grow freely. Opposite, bottom: The more informal area of Hampton Court, rich with flowering shrubs and herbaceous plants (right: foxglove; left: kniphophia).

Where: On the banks of the Thames, at the intersection of the A 308 and the A309, in west London.

Getting there: There are direct trains every half an hour from Waterloo station to Hampton Court station. The trip takes about half an hour, and the gardens are two minutes on foot from the station. Alternatively you can use the underground or the large number of buses available.

Visiting hours: The gardens are open all year round from dawn to dusk.

Information: tel. 0044 20 87819500; fax. 0044 20 87819669; or visit www.hrp.org.uk.

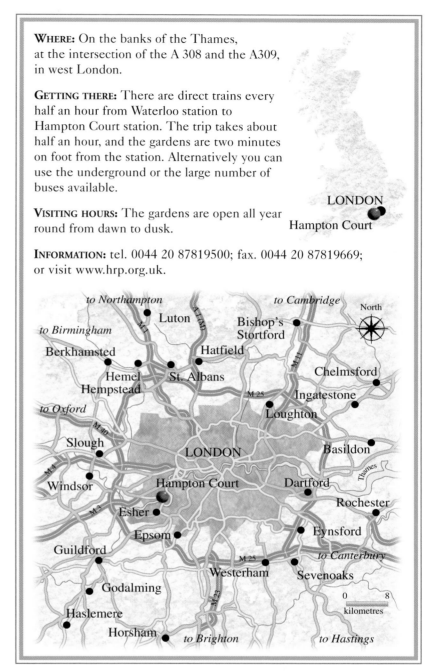

other trees were scattered about to give the garden a vertical dimension.

From this intimate and secluded corner destined for walks, only a labyrinth formed of hedged pathways survives today. The rest of the area has been transformed into an informal garden, which gives its best in spring when the *prunus*, magnolias, primroses and narcissuses flower.

Modification and enhancements also affected the south side of the palace, which had hosted the knot gardens of Henry VIII. In their place, the Privy Garden of William III was created. Enclosed at the bottom by a precious wrought iron gate, at the centre it displayed a large fountain surrounded by elegant grass parterres, which were decorated with yews and hollies trimmed into pyramids in the Dutch style, and to which were added, in good weather, orange trees planted in vases.

A few small gardens were also created for Queen Mary to arrange her favourite flowering plants: from the infinite varieties of *Primula auricula*, cultivated in vases and lined up on a series of wooden shelves, to the collection of exotic plants that she had brought with her from Holland, and that found a new home under the shelter of a glasshouse.

In the area once occupied by these delightful botanical jewels, there are today three 'pond' gardens known as the Lake Gardens, one of which hosts, around a central fountain, a series of dense flowerbeds. Next to it, we find a twentieth-century recreation of Henry VIII's knot garden, with rows that weave miniature boxwood, thyme, lavender and santolina.

Among the marvels of Hampton Court there is also a vine, which was planted in 1769 in a small glasshouse, and which continues to yield an abundance of black grapes.

BIRR CASTLE
In the heart of Ireland, a park that has won Guinness Records; a green jewel of world renown.

For almost four centuries Birr Castle has been the residence of the Earls of Rosse, and the vast park that surrounds it holds many records – five stars in the official list of gardens of historical interest in Ireland, and prestigious prizes for the exceptional characteristics shared among a long list of trees and shrubs. It boasts a 12-metre boxwood hedge, the highest in the world, as well as the 'Leviathan', a gigantic telescope built in 1840 by the Third Earl of Rosse, an astronomy enthusiast. On display on a large lawn, this was once the most powerful telescope in the world, drawing crowds of scientists who arrived at Birr from the four corners of the earth to explore galaxies and nebulas.

The castle – a large, grey, gothic edifice– has changed little since the time of Sir Lawrence Parsons, who in 1620 acquired this property in the heart of Ireland. The park, however, is decidedly different from the kitchen garden and the unpretentious orchard that were planted around the castle in those years. This is thanks to fourteen generations of Parsons, who with patience, dedication and considerable financial resources, have slowly created a green jewel of international renown. Today it is a garden where elegant formal terraces – traced with straight avenues, trimmed hedgerows, topiaries and spectacular hornbeam *berceaux* – blend in with the more natural looking areas arranged according to the theory of the 'wild garden'. It features lakes, water courses, expanses of wild flowers and more than 1,000 species of trees and shrubs, planted at Birr from seeds gathered from every part of the world – from China to Guatemala, from Tibet to Chile and Mexico – in the course of botanical expeditions organised with the financial support and direct participation of several members of the Parsons family.

The formal gardens, designed for the zone closest to the castle, made their appearance at the beginning of the seventeenth century, together with the boxwood hedgerow that has managed to reach such a vertiginous height today. Fifty years later, many hectares of agricultural ground had been transformed into a landscape park equipped with the obligatory: undulating slopes, courses of water and sinuous paths.

The creation of the park took many years to accomplish, with continual modifications and enhancements, in some cases dictated

OPPOSITE: *BIRR CASTLE, AN IMPOSING GOTHIC EDIFICE SURROUNDED BY A PARK OF 50 HECTARES (ABOVE, A ROMANTIC CORNER) BORN OF THE PASSION, COMPETENCE AND FINANCIAL COMMITMENT OF MORE THAN FOURTEEN GENERATIONS OF PARSONS, THE FAMILY THAT ACQUIRED THE ESTATE IN 1620.* TOP: *BRENDAN PARSONS, CURRENT PROPRIETOR AND SEVENTH EARL OF ROSSE.*

LEFT: *CASCADES, JETS AND SUSPENDED BRIDGES CHARAC-TERISE THE SHADY VALLEY, WHICH HOSTS A GARDEN OF VICTORIAN FERNS.* OPPOSITE, BOTTOM: *THE BLUE-VIOLET SCRUB OF A FLOWERING* CEANOTHUS *REJUVINATES THE OLD STONES;* TOP RIGHT: *THE ORIGINAL HORNBEAM* BERCEAU, *ONE OF THE MARVELS OF BIRR CASTLE;* LEFT: *A PATH IN THE PARK, SHADED BY A THICK GALLERY OF BAMBOO.*

by the need to offer work to the local population. The third Earl of Rosse, the one who built the telescope, tried to ease the consequences of the famine that struck Ireland towards the middle of the nineteenth century by entrusting works of extraordinary proportions to hundreds of gardeners.

The arrival of exotic plants – the true glory of Birr – began in the eighteenth century, but only really surged forward in the 1920s, when the sixth Earl of Rosse, a genuine plantsman and enthusiastic collector of botanical specimens, definitively transformed Birr into one of the most famous gardens of Europe. He was supported in this undertaking by his wife Anne, daughter of the owners of Nymans, a much admired garden in the south of England that today is one of the jewels of the National Trust.

Lady Anne, gifted in garden design, remodelled the now run-down boxwood parterre in front of the castle, which had been inspired by a model from the seventeenth century. She created an original and scenic hornbeam *berceau* that became one of the marvels of Birr, with

127

LEFT AND OPPOSITE: *THE FORMAL GARDEN IN FRONT OF THE CASTLE DATES BACK TO THE SEVENTEENTH CENTURY, BUT IT WAS REDESIGNED IN THE 1920S BY LADY ANNE, WIFE OF THE SIXTH EARL OF ROSSE, WHO WAS INSPIRED BY A SEVENTEENTH-CENTURY MODEL. THE BOXWOOD HEDGES THAT FIGURE IN THE GUINNESS BOOK OF RECORDS ARE IN FACT THE HIGHEST IN THE WORLD AT 12 METRES AND ALSO DATE BACK TO THE BEGINNING OF THE EIGHTEENTH CENTURY.*

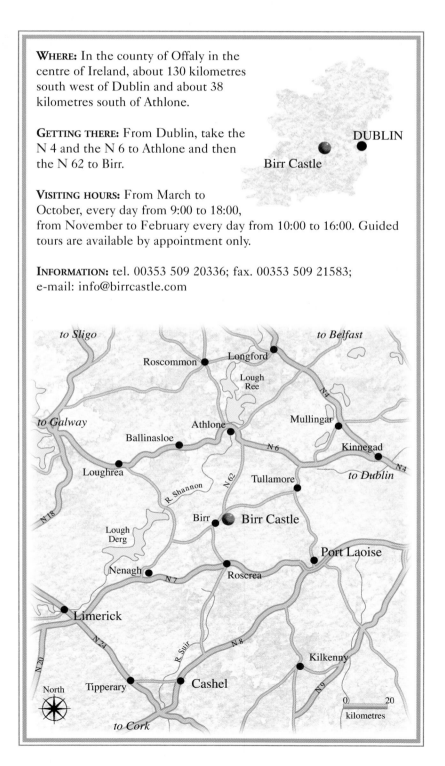

WHERE: In the county of Offaly in the centre of Ireland, about 130 kilometres south west of Dublin and about 38 kilometres south of Athlone.

GETTING THERE: From Dublin, take the N 4 and the N 6 to Athlone and then the N 62 to Birr.

VISITING HOURS: From March to October, every day from 9:00 to 18:00, from November to February every day from 10:00 to 16:00. Guided tours are available by appointment only.

INFORMATION: tel. 00353 509 20336; fax. 00353 509 21583; e-mail: info@birrcastle.com

branches that interweave to form a baroque design. In addition, she decorated corners of the garden with benches and ornaments that still exist today. Lord Michael looked after the plants, finding every possible means to procure the seeds of rare species, especially those originating in the Far East, and arranging them at appropriate points in the garden according to their requirements.

For the last thirty years Birr has been entrusted to the care of Lord Brendan, seventh Earl of Rosse, who, faithful to family tradition, continues to collect precious botanical specimens, Along the banks of the lake and river in the park, or next to the shady valley with its garden of Victorian ferns, little bridges, cascades, jets of water and moss-covered stones, you can admire an extraordinary collection of firs, pines, maples, limes, beeches, horse chestnuts, oaks, cypresses and magnolias. Here you can also find the largest grey poplar in the world, a *Metasequoia glyptostroboides*, which before 1941, when it was discovered in a forest in central China, was only known from the fossil remains of specimens that lived millions of years ago, or marvels like *Ehretia dicksonii*, a very decorative Chinese tree that is covered with white, fragrant flowers in June.

In the formal garden in front of the castle, you can find the most famous plant at Birr – the *Pluripremiata peonia* 'Anne Rosse': a hybrid bred as a result of the horticultural abilities of Lord Michael, who managed to crossbreed a peony discovered in China in 1937 with another found in the mountains of Tibet.

ITALY - SWITZERLAND

VILLA LANTE • NINFA • VILLA TRISSINO MARZOTTO • VILLA SAN REMIGIO • THE BRISSAGO ISLANDS

The exedra in the Garden of Sighs (Villa San Remigio, Italy)

130

VILLA LANTE *One of the best preserved Italian Renaissance gardens, whose water features still fascinate today.*

The garden of Cardinal Giovanni Gambara, built in the second half of the sixteenth century at the foot of the Cimini Mountains in the countryside of Viterbo, was immediately praised and admired for its fountains, judged even more spectacular than those of the famous villa built a few years previously at Tivoli by another Church leader, the Cardinal Ippolito d'Este. There were also a few criticisms however, like that made by the stern Cardinal Carlo Borromeo, who after a visit to the garden of Bagnaia harshly scolded the master of the house for its evident splendour: 'Monsignor, you would have done better to build a monastery with the money that you threw away to build this place'.

Indeed, the powerful Cardinal Gambara, who had obtained possession of this property from Pope Pio V, had not spared any expense to realise the ambitious plans that would increase his already considerable personal prestige, and would transform an insignificant hunting estate built by Raffaele Riario, nephew of Pope Sixtus IV and Bishop of Viterbo from 1498 to 1505, into a garden that would unravel the complex tale of man's relationship with nature.

To reach this end, most of the old wood that covered the area with holm oaks and chestnuts was preserved – its wild appearance made it the perfect symbol of 'untamed nature'. To emphasise this meaning,

several fountains and sculptures were arranged among the ancient trees, though most of these ornaments have now disappeared, such as the Fountain of Bacchus, the Fountain of Lion Cubs, and the Fountain of Acorns – which represented the mythical and happy golden age when animals were docile, wine flowed in rivers and men could draw sustenance without toil from the fruits that Mother Earth offered. Others illustrated instead humanity's descent into decadence over the less fortunate silver, iron, and bronze periods, in which nature grew more hostile until the disaster of the Deluge, represented by a riotous fountain of the same name, which still sprays its water everywhere.

At this point in the story there is a reversal of fortune and a new era begins, characterised by the dominion of art and reason over 'wild' nature, and of which the Cardinal felt a proud protagonist. This triumphant epilogue is demonstrated – today as it was four centuries ago – by an orderly, geometric garden cut out of the woods, timeless and in sharp contrast to the rustic, chaotic surroundings. The designer Jacopo Barozzi (also known as il Vignola), the most famous architect of the period, turned the side of the hill into a terrace as the Italian style prescribed, extracting a sequence of five wide shelves linked by an elegant play of steps and slopes. Barozzi then

LEFT: *THE FRENCH-STYLE PARTERRE ARRANGED ON THE LOWEST OF THE FIVE TERRACES AT THE GARDEN OF VILLA LANTE. FORMED OF BOXWOOD CURLS AGAINST A BACKGROUND OF CLAY DUST, THE PARTERRE WAS REMADE AT THE END OF THE SEVENTEENTH CENTURY. THE ORIGINAL PLAN BY IL VIGNOLA FEATURED TWELVE SQUARE FLOWERBEDS BORDERED BY VIBURNUM HEDGEROWS, WITH FRUIT TREES PLANTED AT REGULAR INTERVALS.* OPPOSITE: *THE FOUNTAIN OF GIANTS* (TOP, DETAIL).

RIGHT: *THE FAMOUS WATER CHAIN, A MINIATURE CASCADE IN WHICH THE STONE BORDERS IMITATE EITHER THE EDDIES OF A MOUNTAIN STREAM, OR THE PINCERS OF A CRAYFISH, CARDINAL GAMBARA'S EMBLEM. THE WATER CHAIN, LIKE THE OTHER FOUNTAINS ARRANGED ON DIFFERENT TERRACES ALONG THE MEDIAL AXIS OF THE GARDEN, IS FED BY WATER FLOWING FROM THE FOUNTAIN BUILT ON THE LEVEL ABOVE, IN THIS CASE THE FOUNTAIN OF THE FLOOD. OPPOSITE: THE FRENCH PARTERRE FROM ANOTHER ANGLE.*

substituted the tangled undergrowth of the wood with evergreen plants – boxwood, yew, oak, laurel, viburnum – trimmed into geometric forms or reduced to the clear outlines of hedgerows, which were far removed from the exuberance of nature. Above all he sought control of water, trapping it in a variety of fountains positioned on different terraces following the medial axis of the garden, where they still offer an unforgettable spectacle.

From the thunderous Fountain of the Deluge, arranged on the highest level and flanked by two pavilions dedicated to the Muses, the water resurfaces in the octagonal Fountain of Dolphins, recalling the passage from the *Metamorphoses* in which Ovid describes these marine mammals leaping among the oak branches during the deluge. Then it flows along a narrow canal between two borders of sculpted stone in the form of crayfish pincers – the owner's emblem – that artistically transform the water into the eddies of a mountain stream. Lower down the water reappears in the monumental Fountain of Giants – representing an allegory of the Arno and the Tiber, the two rivers of Tuscia – and transforms itself into the jets of the Fountain of Lamps, modelled on ancient oil lamps.

ABOVE: *The Fountain of the Moors, built by Cardinal Montalto on the death of the Cardinal Gambara. It lies at the centre of four water parterres, in which miniature military craft float.* RIGHT: *The Fountain of the Giants. The two statues symbolise the Tiber and Arno rivers.* OPPOSITE: *The Fountain of the Dolphins, which takes up a passage of the* Metamorphoses *in which Ovid describes dolphins that invade the woods during the Deluge.*

The French parterre on the lowest terrace – redone at the end of the seventeenth century, after the villa had passed to the Lante della Rovere family (who kept it from 1657 until 1933) – is a little different from the original one designed by il Vignola. This was formed of a series of squares, filled with flowers and surrounded by low borders of *Viburnum tinus* and had fruit trees planted at regular intervals along the hedgerows in order to give the terrace a vertical dimension.

Despite this and other inevitable transformations that took place over the course of the years – during the time of Cardinal Gambara for example, the area of the park close to the Fountain of the Flood was brightened, not only by the sound of water, but by the song issuing from birds in two precious cages – the Renaissance garden of Bagnaia is without doubt among the best preserved gardens of its period.

WHERE: Bagnaia, Latium, about 5 kilometres from Viterbo.

GETTING THERE: From Viterbo take bus no. 6 or 4 from Piazza del Sacrario; by car travel along the road for Soriano nel Cimino.

VISITING HOURS: Every day except Monday, from 8:30 until one hour before sunset.

INFORMATION: tel. 0761 288008.

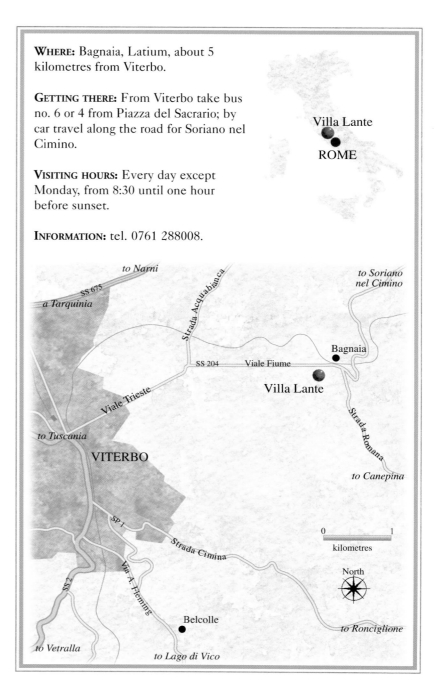

It finally comes to rest in four basins in the lowest part of the garden, which reflect the sky above the triumphant Fountain of the Moors – a feature set in a radiant parterre of boxwood curls against a background of red clay dust. But before it does, the water also animates the open-air lunch room on the terrace situated at the foot of the Fountain of the Giants, by flowing along a groove in the centre of a long peperino table – the so-called 'Cardinal's Table' – a refinement that kept the wine chilled and allowed dishes to flow towards their guests. This was an idea copied from a description by Pliny of a similar table with floating plates, built in his garden in Tuscany.

NINFA
So studied that it appears spontaneous, Ninfa is rich in history, loved by many, and the most beautiful twentieth-century garden in Italy.

In the Roman countryside, at the foot of the Lepini Mountains, botanical treasures and historical ruins weave their unique charm in a garden created a little at a time by the last three generations of Caetani, Dukes of Sarmoneta, an old and noble family that gave birth to popes and cardinals, artists and politicians.

The ruins are those of Ninfa, a village that in medieval times lay in a strategic position on the road that joined Rome to Naples, acquired by the Caetani family in 1298 and completely destroyed a century later in the conflict provoked by the Great Schism. Abandoned by its inhabitants and occasionally frequented by bandits, Ninfa entered a long period of hibernation that lasted until the 1920s, when Ada Caetani fell in love with those eight hectares of ground, with their bramble-covered ruins and crystal-clear rivers, and decided to transform them into a garden. The Duchess's idea was to glorify the romantic character of this mysterious place, respecting nature's work over the centuries as much as possible and substituting only the less attractive wild plants for more suitable ornamental ones.

With the help of her son, Gelasio, an engineering expert, Ada restored unsound ruins and transformed the old city hall into a comfortable country residence. Then she brought back to order the water lock system, which in medieval times controlled the flow of water from a generous spring, and planted holm oaks, cypresses, walnuts, Atlantic cedars and many other trees with tall trunks that still provide pleasant shade, plus a great number of clematis and climbing roses to cover the walls of the ruins in place of the brambles.

In the 1930s after the death of Ada and Gelasio, the garden was passed to the care of his brother, Roffredo, and his wife Marguerite Chapin, a very learned and cultured American from Boston. Roffredo, gifted with an excellent musical ear, designed a series of streams that with their little cascades still fill the garden with the most pleasant murmurs, while Marguerite lengthened the list of plants with hundreds of viburnum, magnolias, camellias, rhododendrons, peonies, lilacs, roses and especially, with flowering

RIGHT AND BELOW: *CASTLE RUINS, BUILDINGS, CHURCHES AND BELL TOWERS STUD THE GARDEN OF NINFA — ALL THAT REMAINS OF A VILLAGE THAT EMERGED DURING THE LATE ROMAN EMPIRE, AND WHICH BECAME STRATEGICALLY IMPORTANT IN MEDIEVAL TIMES. IN 1298 IT WAS ACQUIRED BY THE CAETANI FAMILY, AND REMAINED THEIR PROPERTY EVEN AFTER IT FELL INTO RUIN AND WAS ABANDONED BY ITS INHABITANTS. OPPOSITE: AN APPLE TREE IN FLOWER.*

apple and cherry trees, for which she had a real passion.

Duchess Marguerite also transformed Ninfa into a real intellectual salon, frequented by artists and literati from all over the world. In keeping with her wishes, the garden conformed to the principles of the 'wild garden', with trees and shrubs allowed to grow freely and lawns that were never cut – to permit expanses of forget-me-nots, buttercups, bell flowers, dandelions and many other wild flowers. A

flourishing exuberance reigned throughout, reproducing, on a small scale, the spontaneity of nature.

It was a plan that did not quite appeal to Lelia – Marguerite's daughter, the last representative of the Caetani family, and a capable gardener who gave Ninfa its definitive appearance – and her sense of order. Under her direction, begun in the 1960s, the garden complied with the principle of 'controlled disorder': a space where everything

seemed to happen by accident, but instead where the presence
of every plant, from the most imposing tree to the smallest fern,
followed a careful and well thought-out plan. Lawns were mowed,
the more exuberant trees and shrubs were resized, and the plants
that Marguerite so valued for their messy appearance, like the hazel
trees, were drastically reduced; according to Lelia they compromised
the harmony of the garden.

Like the capable painter she was, Lelia arranged, at appropriate

141

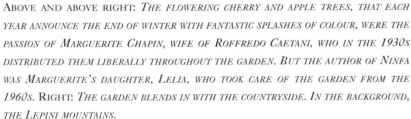

ABOVE AND ABOVE RIGHT: *THE FLOWERING CHERRY AND APPLE TREES, THAT EACH YEAR ANNOUNCE THE END OF WINTER WITH FANTASTIC SPLASHES OF COLOUR, WERE THE PASSION OF MARGUERITE CHAPIN, WIFE OF ROFFREDO CAETANI, WHO IN THE 1930S DISTRIBUTED THEM LIBERALLY THROUGHOUT THE GARDEN. BUT THE AUTHOR OF NINFA WAS MARGUERITE'S DAUGHTER, LELIA, WHO TOOK CARE OF THE GARDEN FROM THE 1960S. RIGHT: THE GARDEN BLENDS IN WITH THE COUNTRYSIDE. IN THE BACKGROUND, THE LEPINI MOUNTAINS.*

spots, a long list of plants capable of yielding flowers with delicate, pastel shades: heather and lavender; clematis; and white, light-yellow and pink roses. She also created original pairings of botanical species, for example bamboo standing out against a carpet of acanthus leaves, red beeches dramatically outlined against dark green cypresses, and Nordic birches arranged next to a radiant *Albizzia julibrissin*. Even the banks of the river were redesigned, with iris, callus, rose bushes, *Cotoneastro* and fotinias blending with the enormous leaves and thorny stems of *Gunnera manicata* – wise choices that created a paradise of harmonious colours, forms, filtered lights and studied perspectives.

Today, hundreds of trees and shrubs follow their natural inclinations, roses and clematises clamber over ancient ruins, and

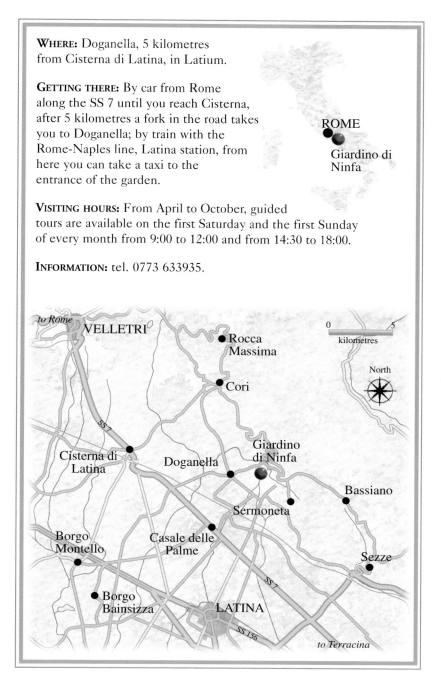

WHERE: Doganella, 5 kilometres from Cisterna di Latina, in Latium.

GETTING THERE: By car from Rome along the SS 7 until you reach Cisterna, after 5 kilometres a fork in the road takes you to Doganella; by train with the Rome-Naples line, Latina station, from here you can take a taxi to the entrance of the garden.

VISITING HOURS: From April to October, guided tours are available on the first Saturday and the first Sunday of every month from 9:00 to 12:00 and from 14:30 to 18:00.

INFORMATION: tel. 0773 633935.

long, drooping clusters of lilac *Wisteria floribunda*, 'Macrobotrys', sweetly brush the waters of the river from a Roman bridge. Fragrances and flowerings alternate continuously throughout the year. At the beginning of spring, blooms as light as snow on the many species of Japanese maples, *Prunus* and *Malus* are arranged in order to be admired from various angles of the garden. These are followed by peony, *Ceanothus*, trumpet-flowers, honeysuckle and above all roses, found amongst a host of bushes, shrubs and climbers that grow everywhere: along avenues, on lawns, walls, and even on a gigantic cypress tree. In autumn you can count on the flaming colours of the maples, while in winter the air is filled with the delicious fragrances of *Lonicera fragrantissima*, calycanthus, witch hazel and *Mahonia*.

VILLA TRISSINO MARZOTTO

One of the most important seventeenth-century gardens from Veneto — a perfect example of the symbiotic relation between art and nature, architecture and landscape.

Looking out over the Agno Valley from above, the castle once dominated much of the grounds that were under the jurisdiction of the Trissino family. In the middle of the medieval period, this fortress stood out imposingly against the summit of the hill – a true symbol of the feudal power in the region. In the centuries that followed, the castle, and the extensive grounds sloping down the side of the hill, met with a series of revisions, until they acquired the appearance that we admire today in the enormous complex of parkland and two villas that is Trissino Marzotto.

The first changes, in 1484 and 1493, transformed the defensive construction with its forbidding appearance into a refined and comfortable residential villa, in keeping with the economic power and the socio-cultural status of the Counts of Trissino. The Counts acquired it because they had good relations with the Republic of Serenissima, which dominated the area from the beginning of the fifteenth century. But it was only from the beginning of 1722 that the property really changed its appearance, when further restructuring was entrusted to the Ticinese architect, Franceso Muttoni. Inspired by the Veneto tradition and the Palladian style, Muttoni developed a garden design admirably suited to the sharp and irregular slope of the grounds. The terraces and belvedere opened harmoniously onto the surrounding landscape offering new and surprising views.

RIGHT: *THE WESTERN FAÇADE OF THE UPPER VILLA, WITH ITS DOUBLE STAIRCASE.* TOP: *THE FOUNTAIN OF NEPTUNE.* OPPOSITE: *THE VIALE DELLE CEDRAIE, BORDERED BY TERRACOTTA POTS CONTAINING LEMON PLANTS, ALTERNATING WITH STATUES REPRESENTING MYTHICAL SUBJECTS – THE WORKS OF ORAZIO MARINALI.*

This perfect symbiosis between nature and art, architecture and landscape, is still the key to Villa Trissino today – that and the impressive restoration carried out after long years of neglect by the current owner, Count Giannino Marzotto. The dialogue between art and nature begins the moment you walk through the top entrance gate in Piazza Gian Giorgio Trissino, overlooked by the parish church of Sant'Andrea and the old stables, which were once a part of the property. The north and west sides of the Upper Villa are covered with virgin vines and ivy up to the top floor.

Turning immediately to the right, into the gravel avenue lined with roses and seasonal flowers, you reach the monumental, eighteenth-century entrance by Muttoni, which gives access to the long formal avenue called 'delle Cedraie', where a row of terracotta vases containing lemon trees interspersed with statues depicting mythological statues (the work of Orazio Marinali) form a counterpoint, typical of formal Italian design. The statues are made from the white stone of Vicenza, which stands out against the backdrop of boxwood on the pathway below: the 'Viale dei Bossi'. A long gallery of yews forms the property boundary. Four powerful cypresses, more than 25 metres high, mark the end of the avenue and the walkway to the octagonal parterre, designed by Muttoni and enhanced by the statues of Marinali.

To the right of the parterre, a descending path leads into the shady calm of the most romantic and informal part of the garden, filled with trees and shrubs: yews, oaks, sequoias, and a magnificent beech, with a wild undergrowth of holly and butcher's broom.

Passing through a relatively new olive grove and a wrought iron gate attributed

RIGHT: WHAT REMAINS OF THE LOWER VILLA.
AFTER GOING UP IN FLAMES TWICE DURING THE
COURSE OF THE NINETEENTH CENTURY, IT WAS
TOTALLY ABANDONED. NOW WITHOUT A ROOF, IT
HAS BEEN COMPLETELY INVADED BY IVY. AT THE
CENTRE OF THE ENORMOUS GARDEN BELOW, ON A
BRIGHT GREEN LAWN, IS AN OCTAGONAL FISH TANK
(ABOVE), DECORATED IN EACH CORNER BY A
STATUE BY MARINALI. OTHER STATUES DOT
THE BALUSTRADE THAT CIRCLES THE LAWN:
FIGURES OF PEASANTS, MUSICIANS AND WOMEN
WITH CHILDREN, HOLDING BUNCHES OF FLOWERS
AND FRUITS.

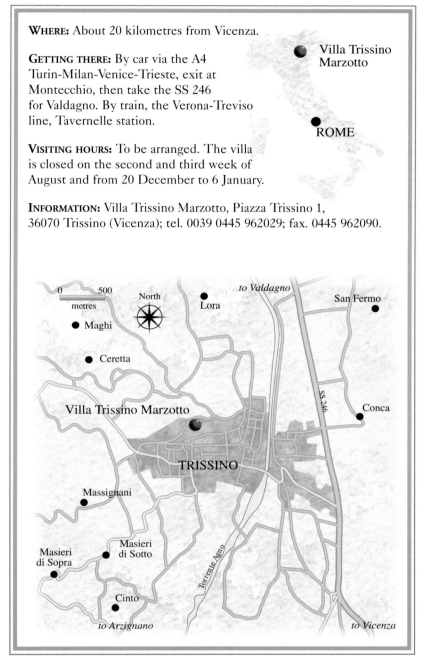

WHERE: About 20 kilometres from Vicenza.

GETTING THERE: By car via the A4 Turin-Milan-Venice-Trieste, exit at Montecchio, then take the SS 246 for Valdagno. By train, the Verona-Treviso line, Tavernelle station.

VISITING HOURS: To be arranged. The villa is closed on the second and third week of August and from 20 December to 6 January.

INFORMATION: Villa Trissino Marzotto, Piazza Trissino 1, 36070 Trissino (Vicenza); tel. 0039 0445 962029; fax. 0445 962090.

to Girolamo Frigimelica, one arrives at the Lower Villa, built by the Trissino del Ramo Riale family (the Trissino Baston family owned the Upper Villa) but struck by lightning in 1841. In 1843, Alessandro Trissino, an amateur romantic architect, transformed the ruins of the villa into a castle of sorts, raising four crenellated towers in the corners of the central body. When it went up in flames a second time, the villa was abandoned; invaded by ivy today, it forms a backdrop to the belvedere terrace below, where a large octagonal water basin – a fish tank – stands out against the lawn, surrounded by a lavender border punctuated in each corner by Marinali statues.

Other statues emphasise the balustrade circling the lawn; more watch from the villa above the double stone staircase: figures of farmers, musicians, hunters and women with children, holding bunches of flowers and fruits, provide animation with their pastoral gestures.

Reflections of the sky in the water, coupled with the whiteness of the stone, confer an extraordinarily bright and airy influence to the first floor, which is framed by hills, lawns, villages, and the woody vegetation on the south east perimeter of the property, reached via a second double staircase. On the floor below, between two arched staircases, there is a fountain dedicated to Neptune, a further example of the statuesque art of the eighteenth century.

From the balustrade that encloses this lawn, one looks out over a large wood of oaks, yews, cypresses, an impressive hornbeam, and onto a wide grassy clearing called the Green Oasis, used for country fairs. Around this lawn, there are more statues with allegorical themes: the continents, the seasons and the character of man.

VILLA SAN REMIGIO *Inspired by the*
Italian Baroque style, a garden born to celebrate feelings and emotions.

'Here we lie: Silvio and Sofia Della Valle di Casanova, on the spot where our childhood united us, in this garden born of a youthful vision: as adolescents we dreamt it; as man and wife we realised it.' These words, engraved on a tombstone in the square in front of Villa San Remigio, hold the history of one of the most fascinating gardens in Castagnola – a triangle of hilly ground once covered with a wood of chestnut trees (hence the name), which extends into the waters of Lake Maggiore between Intra and Pallanza. Here, from the end of the eighteenth century, the proprietors built villas and gardens, which were soon crowded with a host of visitors: from Turin, Milan, Naples, as well as England, Ireland, Germany, etc. – all fascinated by the scene they encountered during their Grand Tour. Of these, the Brownes from Ireland and the Della Valle di Casanovas from Naples, who were

related by marriage, acquired a considerable number of plots between 1859 and 1890, which were then unified into one property.

The history of Villa San Remigio begins in 1896, the year in which Marquis Silvio Della Valle di Casanova and his cousin, Sofia Browne, celebrated their marriage. As a learned and cultured couple, he a poet and musician, she a painter and competent botanist, they began to build, in place of the pseudo-Swiss chalet that Sofia's grandfather wanted, an elegant villa in the Neapolitan baroque style. They then began an enormous project of works on the garden, which lasted for twenty years and radically changed the appearance of Castagnola. We can still see the result: a garden completely in harmony with the surrounding countryside, with abundant allusions to the Italian baroque style – from the arrangement of the parterres, the scenic views, the

RIGHT: *THE SPECTACULAR PANORAMA OF LAKE MAGGIORE, WHICH YOU CAN ENJOY FROM THE BALCONY OF VILLA SAN REMIGIO.* TOP: *A FLOWERING TAMARISK IN THE GOLDEN GARDEN.* OPPOSITE: *THE GARDEN OF JOY WITH ITS THREE CENTRAL FLOWERBEDS, COLUMNS, BOXWOOD HEDGES AND THE BASIN IN WHICH A HORSE-DRAWN CARRIAGE MADE OF SHELLS TRANSPORTS THE NYMPH GALATEA.*

ABOVE: *A FOUNTAIN-NICHE IN THE GARDEN OF JOY AMONG ORDERLY BOXWOOD HEDGEROWS AND AN EXUBERANT AZALEA AMOENA IN FLOWER. THE SLENDER, PERFECTLY CYLINDRICAL TRUNKS BELONG TO PALM TREES, AN EXOTIC NECESSITY IN THE LAKE GARDENS OF THE NINETEENTH CENTURY. RIGHT: WHITE AZALEAS IN THE GARDEN OF SIGHS. OPPOSITE: THE GRAND STAIRCASE, COVERED WITH MOSS AND LICHEN, WHICH LEADS TO THE GARDEN OF MELANCHOLY.*

different shades of green; on the bottom wall, completing this solemn scene, you can make out an aedicule (temple) covered with mosaic pieces in two colours, with three niches animated by sculptures – one of which is a monumental Hercules killing the Hydra of Lerna, a work by the revered Giovanni Marchiori from Veneto. At the centre is a water basin with four stone shells and the emerging figure of a nymph or a goddess. All around, the tall and stately conifers, boxwoods and camphors emphasise the melancholy atmosphere.

After a few steps you reach the Garden of Joy, ruled by the nymph Galatea – graceful and elegant in her carriage formed of shells and drawn by two horses. The basin rises between the elegant designs of boxwood flowerbeds. Overlooking this garden bordered by jasmine is the glasshouse where Marquise Sofia tended begonias – plants that love the shade and humidity; she would bed them directly on rocks so that a stream of water could keep them moist even in the summer.

The Garden of Joy is followed by the Golden Garden, dedicated to

obelisks, the statues and the staircases, to the meticulous choice of names for each of the 'rooms' in which the garden was divided. Names inspired by the feelings so central to Villa San Remigio; faithful mirrors of a romantic culture, tinged with melancholy and consumed by the passions experienced by the sensitive authors of these marvels.

One of the rooms, for example, is called the Garden of the Melancholy: shady, severe, without a single flower, yet playing on

the inexorable passing of time, reflected in the big, stone-sculpted sundial on the grounds. And finally, to complete this evocative series, the Garden of Sighs and the Garden of Memories. The first, a nostalgic hymn to past times, consists of a belvedere and an enormous exedra with seven niches hosting statues that reflect mythological themes. The second contains a wide basin with simple lines, obelisks, columns and figures of cupid wrapped in climbing roses extolling the beauty of the ephemeral in contrast to eternal love. The Garden of Memories is overlooked by an unusual building, a Romanesque church with many apses: the studio of Sofia Della Valle di Casanova, where she withdrew to paint, enjoying the natural light that fell from a window above.

The Italian gardens blend harmoniously with the woody area of the garden and with the interior English park – from which a winding path leads to the villa, leaving behind it the majestic entrance hall guarded by two lions, seated on top of two columns holding the shield with the emblem of the Della Valle di Casanove family. In the park Marquise Sofia introduced plants that were little known at the time, plants that arrived from Japan, South America and other distant countries, and which still converse happily with the local ones today.

ABOVE: *In the foreground, the Garden of Melancholy, with the central fountain dominated by a figure of a nymph. In the background, the façade of the villa in the Neapolitan baroque style. Opposite, bottom: The studio of Marquise Sofia Della Valle di Casanova, who was a capable painter. Opposite, top left: Against a background of azaleas and rhododendrons, the staircase leading to the Garden of Sighs; top right: A glimpse of the Garden of Joy.*

WHERE: Verbania Pallanza, on the Piedmontese bank of Lake Maggiore.

GETTING THERE:
From Milan and Turin via highway A6, exit at Gravellona/Verbania, then follow the SS 34 in the direction of the Swiss border; by train via the Milan-Domodossola/Ginevra-Berna line; from the Verbania station square, you can reach San Remigio by taxi or by bus.

VISITING HOURS: Guided tours are available in the spring-summer period, but only by reservation.

INFORMATION: Ufficio del Turismo, c.so Zanitello 6/8, Verbania Pallanza; tel. 0323 503249.

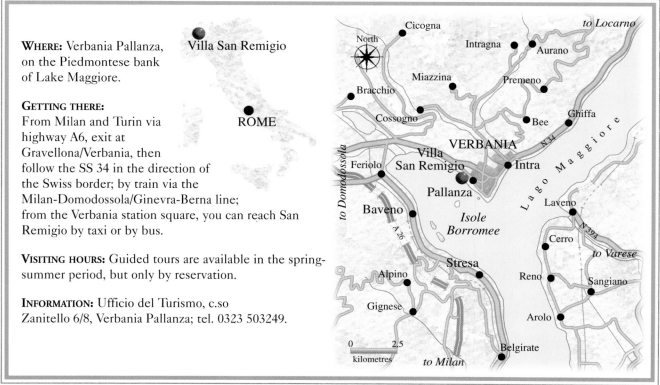

THE BRISSAGO ISLANDS *One*
island is a little trove of natural flora, the other hosts an important botanical park.

Thanks to the zeal of a Russan noblewoman who led a life filled with adventure and many lovers, a tiny archipelago of Lake Maggiore has been transformed into a beautiful botanical park where, despite an unfavourable latitude, many plant species from the warm zones of the world flourish.

The lady was Antoniette de Saint-Léger: intelligent and very beautiful, born in 1856 in Russia to enterprising parents who, despite their modest origins, frequented the court of the Tsar. Sent to Italy at a very young age because the humid, cold Russian winters were cruel to her unhealthy lungs, the charming Antoniette not only discovered the warm Italian sun, but three husbands. The first two marriages only lasted a few months, but the third, to the rich Irish Baron, Richard de Saint-Léger, was decidedly more stable.

In 1885 the married couple, who had decided to move to the Canton Ticino, bought two small islands in the Swiss part of Lake Maggiore – San Pancrazio and San Apollinare. At the end of the fourteenth century, these were occupied by a convent of the Umiliati Brothers, but from the middle of the sixteenth century, when they were sold to the City of Brissago, they were only populated by rabbits and hunters. Struck by the wild beauty of the area and the mild climate, the baroness first had a villa built on the largest island, and then addressed the greenery. Her plan was to create an area similar to that which had been achieved a few years previously near Ventimiglia by Thomas Hanbury: an aesthetically pleasing garden, but also a place where she could realise a dream: to have delicate, exotic plants, which in the icy countries of Northern Europe could only survive in the warmth of glasshouses, grow out in the open.

As the local vegetation on the smaller island continued to grow undisturbed, the larger one was transformed into a splendid and unusual park, enhanced by a long list of tropical plants that the Baroness had sent to her from all over the world, and that, lovingly tended, managed to adapt to the extraordinarily mild microclimate of the lake. Eucalyptus arrived from Australia; agaves from Mexico; hibiscus, bamboo, arboreal ferns (*Dicksonia antarctica*); poppies from California (*Romneya coulteri*) and palms of all types: from the American *Brahea armata* to the Chinese *Trachycarpus fortunei* and the *Phoenix canariensis*, which originates in the Canary Islands. On the island there was also a large population of Mediterranean scrub, still in excellent health: from cork oaks (*Quercus suber*) and strawberry trees (*Arbutus unedo*), to myrtle, lentisks, rockroses and rosemary.

Once the marriage with Baron Richard was over too, Antoniette continued to live on her beloved island surrounded by painters, sculptors, musicians and writers, making Brissago one of the most lively cultural centres of Europe. But by 1927, Antoniette was short of money and was forced to sell the house and garden to Max Emden, a rich German industrialist, who had the whole villa redone,

ABOVE: *VIEW OF LAKE MAGGIORE FROM THE ISLAND OF SAN PANCRAZIO, ONCE A PRIVATE ESTATE, TODAY THE BOTANICAL PARK OF CANTON TICINO. OPPOSITE, TOP: THE SWISS COAST AND THE TOWN OF BRISSAGO. LEFT: A BALD CYPRESS, ONE OF THE NUMEROUS EXOTIC SPECIES HOSTED BY THE BOTANICAL PARK. OPPOSITE, BOTTOM: AN AERIAL VIEW OF THE TWO ISLANDS OF BRISSAGO, SAN PANCRAZIO (THE BIGGER ONE) AND SAN APOLLINARE, WITH ITS INDIGENOUS VEGETATION.*

155

RIGHT AND OPPOSITE, TOP: *THE* TAXODIUM DISTICHUM, *COMMONLY KNOWN AS BALD CYPRESSES OR* VIRGINIAN CYPRESSES, *ARE TREES ABOUT FORTY METRES HIGH, ORIGINATING IN THE UNITED STATES. THEY USUALLY GROW IN MARSHY, AIRLESS EARTH AND FOR THIS REASON ARE ENDOWED WITH 'RESPIRATORY ROOTS' CALLED PNEUMATOPHORES. THESE RISE VERTICALLY FROM THE WATER AND ABSORB OXYGEN ACROSS SMALL APERTURES (PNEUMATODI), TRANSPORTING IT TO THE SUBMERGED ROOTS. THE BALD CYPRESSES ASSUME A LOVELY RUSTY COLOUR IN AUTUMN.* OPPOSITE, BOTTOM: *AN ARBOREAL FERN (*DICKSONIA ANTARCTICA).

considering it too modest for his sybarite tastes. Fortunately, he did not alter the green spaces, judging these exotic treasures an ideal frame for his opulent lifestyle.

At the beginning of the 1950s, the Brissago Islands again changed hands and were bought by the State of Canton Ticino, which decided to declare the gardens a botanical park. The plant heritage increased and many species were added to the rare list collected by Antoniette, for example *Brachychiton acerifolius*, a tree from the tropical forests of Australia, carrying different forms of leaves on the same plant – simple and oval, or palmate with three or five lobes – and coral red corymbs. Or *Tetracentron sinense*, which lives in the forests of the Himalayas and south-west China, with ear spikes of tiny yellow flowers in summer and dark green leaves that turn a lovely rusty colour in autumn.

The botanical park of Brissago, a precious reserve of biodiversity, includes several plants that are now extinct elsewhere: *Franklinia alatamaha*, a large shrub originating in North America, which is covered in white, fragrant flowers at the beginning of autumn, or

Sophora toromiro, a species of the Leguminose family, which grew wild on the Island of Pasqua.

Scientific interests did not lessen aesthetic concerns, though. The Park of San Pancrazio continues to be exactly as it was during the time of Baroness de Saint-Léger, admired in every season: for the spectacular stretches of azaleas, camellias and rhododendrons, which create bright splashes of colour in the spring; for the snow-white bract, which hangs like little handkerchiefs from the branches in May; for *Davidia involucrata*, a tree that originates in China; and for the fiery autumn colour of the bald cypresses (*Taxodium distichum*) from the United States, with their curious roots protruding from the water.

ABOVE: *A FOUNTAIN INSTALLED RECENTLY IN THE BOTANICAL PARK OF CANTON TICINO, THE WORK OF THE ARTIST REMO ROSSI. OPPOSITE, TOP: HIBISCUS COCCINEUS (RIGHT) AND BEGONIA EVANSIANA; BOTTOM: HIBISCUS MILITARIS (LEFT) AND PALMS. THERE ARE AROUND 1,500 SPECIES OF PLANTS ON THE ISLAND OF SAN PANCRAZIO, MANY OF WHICH ORIGINATE IN TROPICAL COUNTRIES. THE MILD CLIMATE, DUE TO THE MITIGATING FACTOR OF THE LAKE WATER AND THE SHELTER OF NEIGHBOURING MOUNTAINS, HAS PERMITTED ALL THESE PLANTS TO ADAPT AND SURVIVE PERFECTLY.*

WHERE: The Brissago islands are in the Swiss part of Lake Maggiore.

GETTING THERE: Is only possible across the lake, with ferries from Porto Ronco, Locarno or Ascona, or by taxiboat from Porto Ronco or from Ascona.

VISITING HOURS: From March to October, every day from 9:00 to 5:00.

INFORMATION: tel. 0041 91 7914361; fax. 0041 91 7910763; e-mail: dic-isole.brissago@ti.ch

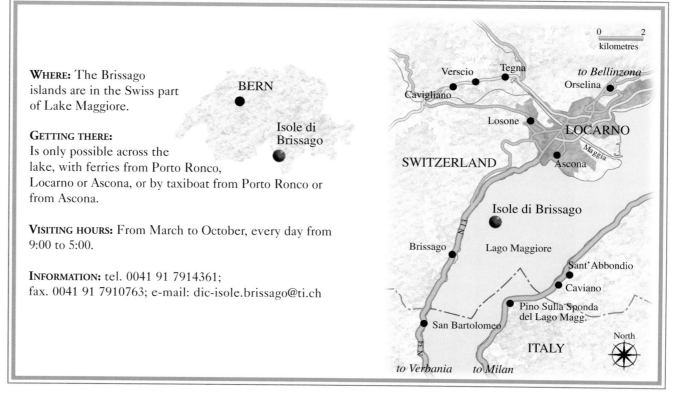

SCANDINAVIA

ROSENDAL PARK

(NORWAY)

160

BARONIET ROSENDAL *In the harsh country of the Great North, a garden where some 2,000 varieties of roses flower.*

A Renaissance garden and a nineteenth-century landscape park in happy cohabitation, impeccably preserved, lie next to a castle set between a steep mountain and the narrow inlet of a fjord. Their history begins with the early ancestors of one of the most powerful families of Danish nobility, the Rosenkrantzs, at a time when they had been reduced to poverty. In 1650, Ludvig Rosenkrantz had the fortune to marry Karen Mowatt, the richest Nordic heiress of the period. Thus he moved to Hatteberg on the south-west coast of Norway, to an agricultural estate acquired immediately after the marriage, where he built a new residence. Considered a luxurious castle among the modest buildings of the area, it was in reality only a solid, comfortable home made of stone, composed of three wings and a wall that protected it from polar winds.

Although there were points on this vast estate that were close to built-up areas and towns, the castle was built in an extremely remote area and, moreover, facing toward the looming outline of the mountain, instead of towards the infinitely brighter marine panorama. This was a bizarre choice that went against the grain, not due to any predeliction for that pictureque landscape (which would only truly be valued many years later at the height of the romantic era), but due to the owner's desire to make a statement. With this castle, Ludvig could face his friends – including his snobby cousins in Copenhagen – with his head held high. They were all owners of sumptuous castles with breathtaking views, but none could boast a spectacular mountain view!

While the building was built in the baroque style that was gaining

RIGHT: *THE KITCHEN GARDENS OF ROSENDAL: RESERVED FOR THE CULTIVATION OF VEGETABLES AND FRUIT TREES, ESPECIALLY APPLE, CHERRY AND PEAR TREES – FAVOURITES IN THE RELATIVELY TEMPERATE CLIMATE THAT THE HARDANGER FJORD ENJOYS. OPPOSITE AND TOP: ROSES, THE MAIN FEATURE OF THE ORNAMENTAL GARDEN.*

CREATED AROUND 1850, ABOUT 200 YEARS AFTER THE CASTLE AND GARDEN, THE ENGLISH-STYLE PARK REACHES THE FOOT OF THE MOUNTAIN THAT TOWERS OVER THE ESTATE. CROWDED WITH TREES, DOTTED WITH PATHS, LAKES AND STREAMS, IT HOSTS A NEOGOTHIC TOWER (RIGHT) AND A SERIES OF WOODEN HOUSES THAT EMPHA-SISE ITS ROMANTIC CHARACTER. SOME OF THE ROOFS ARE COVERED IN GRASS AND SHRUBS (OPPOSITE, BELOW).

popularity across Europe, the garden was designed along already outdated Renaissance lines, completely independently of the house – there was no passageway between the two environments, as was typical of many medieval and First Renaissance gardens. It was divided with a network of intersecting avenues into twelve equally-sized flowerbeds, where ornamental plants were reduced to the minimum – a few flowers and above all boxwood and privet for hedges and borders – while a lot of space was left for vegetables, aromatic herbs and fruit trees. In a corner there was the inevitable basin for a fish tank – evidently indispensable even in an area a stone's throw away from a fjord full of fish.

Fortunately the desire for novelty never encouraged Ludvig Rosenkrantz's successors to modify the design of this garden, which has therefore preserved its original layout. With the years, only the plants changed, substituted some time ago by almost 2,000 varieties of roses, which bloom in the old flowerbeds from July to November.

Towards 1850, to conform to new gardening trends, the owners of Rosendal created a large romantic park, which extends from the house up to the sides of the mountain, and which includes a small, steep and rocky valley crowded with stately trees, crossed by sinuous paths, as well as streams surmounted by rustic bridges. In a shady corner of this park there is a mysterious neogothic tower, an old forge

that seems to come out of the world of fairytales, picturesque stretches of water, and a spectacular natural cascade that forms a background to the park. Visual corridors were created among the trees to capture the marvels of the landscape: the fjord, the cascade, and that looming mountain, harsh and wild, which finally supported the aesthetic mores of the period.

The gardens of the Rosendal castle remained in Danish hands for centuries. In 1927, the by then deserted property was donated to the University of Oslo, which opened it to the public after an accurate restoration.

THE ORNAMENTAL GARDEN, WITH ITS RENAISSANCE LAYOUT, CONSISTS OF TWELVE FLOWERBEDS OF EQUAL SIZE (OPPOSITE, ABOVE), WITH BOXWOOD AND PRIVET BORDERS AND ALMOST 2,000 VARIETIES OF ROSES. ABOVE AND ABOVE RIGHT: THE ROSE PARTERRE. OPPOSITE, BOTTOM: THE CASTLE SEEN FROM THE PARK; RIGHT: THE FAÇADE WITH CLIMBING ROSES AROUND THE WINDOWS OF A WOODEN HOUSE.

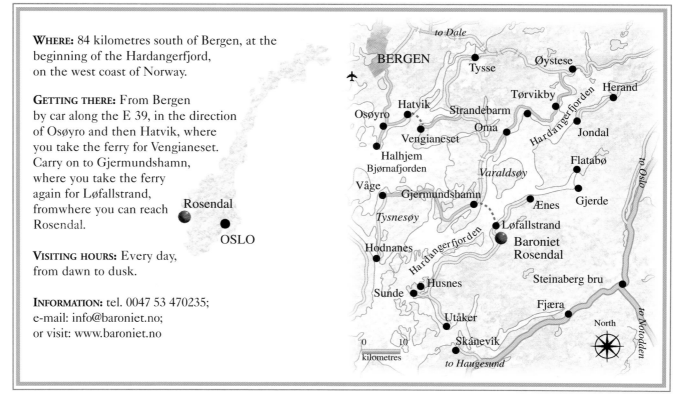

WHERE: 84 kilometres south of Bergen, at the beginning of the Hardangerfjord, on the west coast of Norway.

GETTING THERE: From Bergen by car along the E 39, in the direction of Osøyro and then Hatvik, where you take the ferry for Vengianeset. Carry on to Gjermundshamn, where you take the ferry again for Løfallstrand, fromwhere you can reach Rosendal.

VISITING HOURS: Every day, from dawn to dusk.

INFORMATION: tel. 0047 53 470235; e-mail: info@baroniet.no; or visit: www.baroniet.no

DROTTNINGHOLM *Partly formal garden, partly landscape park – with a touch of madness…*

At the end of the sixteenth century King Johan III of Sweden built a comfortable palace on an island in Lake Mälaren and then presented it as a gift to his beloved consort, Queen Catherine. For this reason the residence was called 'Drottningholm', which means 'Island of the Queen'. Destroyed by a fire in 1661, the palace was immediately restored by the architect, Nicodemus Tessin, commissioned by Queen Hedwig Eleonora to create a summer palace worthy of the important political role assumed by Sweden after the signing of the Peace of Westphalia, which had ended the Thirty Years War.

The royal palace was arranged on a slightly raised level above the lake, to take advantage of the surrounding landscape. It was enhanced by a green space that has preserved its baroque design very well – laid out along a central axis with two types of parterre: a *parterre de broderie* right next to the palace as custom required, with an elegant central fountain and a flowery border dotted with shrubs trimmed into geometric shapes; and immediately beyond this, an elegant water parterre, with a harmonious arrangement of fountains, and basins – round and oval. The parterres were also enhanced by a host of bronze statues created by Adriaen de Vries, a Dutch sculptor who was the student of Giambogna, acquired as the spoils of war from the

OPPOSITE, TOP: *DETAIL OF THE COAT OF ARMS OF THE SWEDISH SOVEREIGNS, WHO STILL LIVE IN PART OF THE PALACE; BOTTOM: THE ENGLISH-STYLE PARK CREATED IN 1780 FOR KING GUSTAV III, WHERE LAKES, CANALS AND ANCIENT TREES ALTERNATE WITH SWEEPING LAWNS.*

ABOVE: *THE BAROQUE GARDEN RIGHT IN FRONT OF THE ROYAL PALACE. IT IS SURROUNDED ON THREE SIDES BY A LONG AVENUE LINED WITH A DOUBLE ROW OF YEWS. LEFT: THE EXTRAVAGANT CONSTRUCTION THAT LOOKS LIKE A CHINESE MILITARY TENT, HIDDEN IN THE GREEN PARK.*

169

FOLLIES? OR THE MEANS TO AMAZE GUESTS?

From the mid-eighteenth century, Chinese pagodas, gothic towers, druidic menhirs, tartar curtains and Egyptian pyramids became indispensable presences in the green spaces of large, aristocratic European residences. Appropriately arranged, these follies had steadily replaced the austere false ruins that populated the first landscape parks; inevitable resting points on garden walks. They enhanced the view, captured the gaze, affirmed the cultural solidity of the owner and above all evoked astonishment and emotion among visitors, transporting them to distant places and distant times. From Moldavian houses to Peruvian cabins, Lapp shelters to Caucasian palaces, the imaginations of owners were limitless when it came to collecting unusual miniature monuments capable of transforming gardens into well-stocked open-air libraries. Most common were the eastern-style constructions, emblems of the fabulous gardens of the Celestial Emperor that were gaining popularity following the accounts of missionaries and travellers: large and small pavilions expressing the period's passion for chinoiserie. In some cases, like at Drottningholm, they were luxuriously decorated on the inside with paintings, carpets, furniture and porcelain imported from the Far East.

garden of Albrecht von Wallenstein in Prague.

The two parterres were then framed by a scenic avenue flanked by the double row of yews that still separate this formal, French-style area from the vast landscape park designed in 1780 for King Gustav III, where sweeping lawns alternate with trees, canals, irregular bodies of water and a bizarre construction that looks like a Chinese military tent. This was a folly, testimony to a passion for the Far East that had begun to take hold in the years around 1750, when Queen Louisa Ulrica had enhanced Drottningholm with a small Chinese village called Canton, arranged in the middle of a thick curtain of fir trees to keep it continually shaded and so emphasise its mysterious allure. Of this bizarre complex only a small building with red lacquered walls and a tiny two-storey pavilion have been preserved. The pavilion – La Confiance – allowed the sovereigns and their guests to eat in peace away from indiscreet eyes because the table, although laid on the ground floor, was raised by means of an ingenious elevator to the dining room on the first floor.

LEFT: THE GARDEN OF DROTTNINGHOLM IS LAPPED BY THE WATERS OF LAKE MÄLAREN, WHICH HAS A SURFACE AREA OF 1,140 KM² AND IS DOTTED WITH 280 ISLANDS. OPPOSITE, BOTTOM: THE LITTLE CHINESE BUILDING, TESTIMONY TO A FASCINATION WITH THE FAR EAST THAT TOOK HOLD IN SWEDEN IN THE MID-EIGHTEENTH CENTURY. BELOW: ONE OF THE FOUNTAINS THAT CONSTITUTE THE WATER PARTERRE NEXT TO THE PARTERRE DE BRODERIE. THE BAROQUE GARDEN WAS DESIGNED BY ARCHITECT NICODERMUS TESSIN AND BUILT BY QUEEN HEDWIG ELEONORA. BOTTOM LEFT: THE ROYAL COAT OF ARMS IN FRONT OF THE PALACE.

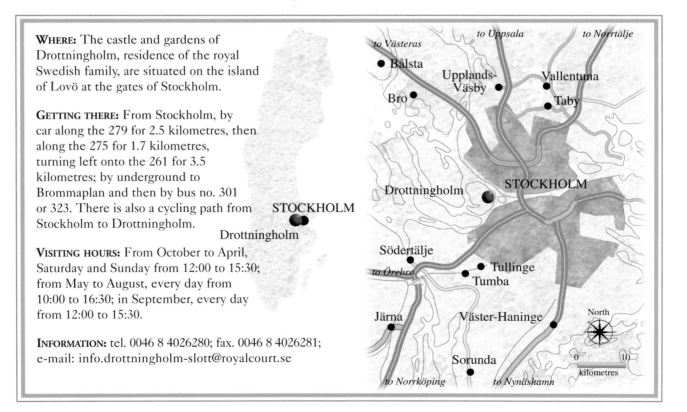

WHERE: The castle and gardens of Drottningholm, residence of the royal Swedish family, are situated on the island of Lovö at the gates of Stockholm.

GETTING THERE: From Stockholm, by car along the 279 for 2.5 kilometres, then along the 275 for 1.7 kilometres, turning left onto the 261 for 3.5 kilometres; by underground to Brommaplan and then by bus no. 301 or 323. There is also a cycling path from Stockholm to Drottningholm.

VISITING HOURS: From October to April, Saturday and Sunday from 12:00 to 15:30; from May to August, every day from 10:00 to 16:30; in September, every day from 12:00 to 15:30.

INFORMATION: tel. 0046 8 4026280; fax. 0046 8 4026281; e-mail: info.drottningholm-slott@royalcourt.se

SPAIN - PORTUGAL

ALHAMBRA • LA GRANJA • FRONTEIRA PALACE

Fronteira Palace (Lisbon, Portugal)

172

ALHAMBRA *The famous Moorish gardens of Europe, where the music of water accompanies the play of light and shade.*

In the sensual Spanish gardens built, from the beginning of the eighteenth century, by Arab conquerors, the fragrance of rose and jasmine blends with the calming green of cypress, myrtle, citrus and pomegranate trees. There are elegant white marble columns, walls covered with painted stuccoes, majolica – the black and white pebbles that form elaborate, geometric designs on the floors – and water is everywhere: in spouting fountains, canals and water basins of all sizes that reflect the blue sky.

Indeed, for a culture forced to live in arid, sun-drenched lands, water provided the greatest of pleasures, a contrast to the harshness of the desert, a truly divine gift. It was indispensable in gardens, which were considered earthly anticipations of the paradise promised by Mohamed and, for this reason, places of delight, light and shade, filled with flowers, fruits, colours, sounds and fragrances.

Pools, canals and fountains of all kinds are central to Alhambra, a fortified citadel built in the fourteenth century by Emir Yusuf I, and then by his son Muhammed V, on a hill with red earth (*Al-Hamra in Arabic means 'red fort'*). Overlooking the sunny plains of Granada, it provides breathtaking views of the mountains – perpetually covered by snow from Sierra Nevada. In this magnificent residence, the plants, water, stuccoes, majolica and other precious architectural features were arranged in a series of inner courtyards. An articulated succession of open-air environments, cosy, intimate and strictly geometrical, these were overlooked by the rooms of the palaces, which were sometimes

OPPOSITE: *THE CITADEL OF ALHAMBRA, WHICH DOMINATES THE PLAINS OF GRANADA FROM ABOVE; TOP: PAINTED STUCCOES DECORATE THE INTERIORS OF PALACES AND COURTYARDS.*

RIGHT: *THE PATIO OF MYRTLES. EVEN HERE THE PRINCIPAL FEATURE OF INTEREST IS THE LONG RECTANGULAR POOL, SURROUNDED BY MARBLE COLUMNS.* BELOW: *IN THE ROOMS AND COURTYARDS OF ALHAMBRA THE OPENINGS TOWARD THE EXTERIOR WERE DESIGNED TO ENCOURAGE SUGGESTIVE GLIMPSES OF THE GARDEN.*

OPPOSITE: *THE GARDENS OF GENERALIFE, PRIVATE RESIDENCE OF THE SULTAN, ADJACENT TO ALHAMBRA. THE PATIO OF CANALS* (LEFT), *WITH A RIBBON OF WATER THAT FLOWS BETWEEN ROSES, OLEANDERS, MYRTLES AND TWO ROWS OF JETS. THE PLANTS, INCLUDING THE CYPRESSES SCULPTED INTO ARCADES* (RIGHT), *ARE NOT ORIGINAL, BUT THE RESULT OF A RESTORATION REALISED IN THE FIRST HALF OF THE TWENTIETH CENTURY.*

also connected to each other by small openings or narrow corridors that allowed one to glimpse the next enclosure.

For example, the Patio of Myrtles, at the centre of the royal reception rooms, is a rectangular space, 37 metres long and 24 metres wide, inundated by sun, paved with white marble tiles and almost entirely occupied by a long water basin bordered by perfectly trimmed, espaliered myrtle. Rigorous and pithy in its design, yet overflowing with architectural decorations, the gaze was directed towards the royal pavilion, from which the sultan, seated on his precious throne with a stretch of water laid out at his feet like a carpet, could cast his eyes over the guests.

The most famous area of Alhambra can be found instead at the centre of what were once the private apartments of the sultan. The austere Patio of Lions is surrounded by an elegant arcade covered with pierced stuccoes that cast their intricate shadows on the walls and a forest of white marble columns. At the time it also hosted a

small garden with plants and flowers, but today the natural universe is represented only by water, which flows from the fountain at the centre of the patio – a white, marble basin supported by twelve lions and considered one of the best examples of Moorish sculpture – along four narrow canals dug into the floor and then to the interior rooms and pavilions that flank it – a fresh, calm murmur.

As well as the Patio of Lions, where there were probably once houses for important court officials, water is also the main feature of the delightful Garden of the Partal: a large rectangular pool of still water is surrounded by palms, cypresses, boxwood hedges and flowery borders, reflecting the façade formed by the arcade (*partal* in Arabic means 'portico') of the Ladies' Tower, a building that boasts decorations older than Alhambra itself.

The continuous music of a subtle stream of water and the changeable play of light and shade make another much admired jewel unforgettable – the Patio of Lindaraja, a tiny enclave

RIGHT: *THE SMALL, REFINED PATIO OF LINDARAJA, ENCLOSED BY A RING OF CYPRESSES AND PLACED BELOW THE LEVEL OF THE PALACE SO THAT ONE CAN ADMIRE IT FROM ABOVE. AT THE CENTRE, A SPOUTING FOUNTAIN. WATER, IN THE FORM OF CANALS, POOLS AND FOUNTAINS (ABOVE) IS THE PRINCIPAL FEATURE OF ALHAMBRA.*

In contrast to the many other palaces built by the Arabs in the course of their long domination of the Iberian peninsula, the Alhambra and the Generalife were not razed to the ground when they were reclaimed by King Ferdinand and Queen Isabella.

In this way they managed to win the battle against time, keeping their original architectural design and the form of the pools and fountains almost unaltered, and only differing from the original in the types of plants that they used. They therefore still manage to recreate the fantastic wealth of colours and fragrances of a past era thanks to a wise restoration that ended in the first half of the twentieth century and that introduced perfectly trimmed boxwood and myrtle hedgerows, galleries of roses and oleanders, cypresses sculpted into arcades and beds full of plants and flowers.

ABOVE: *THE PATIO OF LIONS, THE SMALLEST AND RICHEST OF THE ALHAMBRA COURTYARDS, WHICH TAKES ITS NAME FROM THE CENTRAL FOUNTAIN, A WHITE MARBLE BASIN SUPPORTED BY TWELVE LIONS (OPPOSITE, TOP) SURROUNDED BY ELEGANT COLUMNS, PROVIDING ACCESS TO WHAT WERE ONCE THE APARTMENTS OF THE SULTAN.*

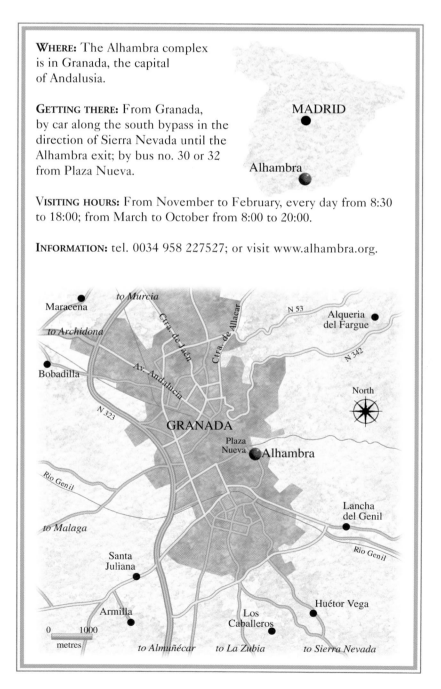

WHERE: The Alhambra complex is in Granada, the capital of Andalusia.

GETTING THERE: From Granada, by car along the south bypass in the direction of Sierra Nevada until the Alhambra exit; by bus no. 30 or 32 from Plaza Nueva.

VISITING HOURS: From November to February, every day from 8:30 to 18:00; from March to October from 8:00 to 20:00.

INFORMATION: tel. 0034 958 227527; or visit www.alhambra.org.

decorated with boxwood hedges and protected by tall cypresses, the only plant decorations that do not belong to the period of this place.

More intimate and refined are the Gardens of Generalife (*Jinan al-Arif meaning 'Gardens of the Overseer' in Arabic*), the residence where the sultan took refuge in summer or when he wanted to escape the formalities of court life, and connected to Alhambra by a long avenue of cypresses. Here, given the private, exclusive character of these green spaces, the stuccoes, majolica and other precious architectural features have been minimized to make room for an abundance of plants and flowers, which add their delightful colours and fragrances to the relaxing murmurs of the ever-present water. In the Patio of Canals, for example, cypresses, oranges and flowerbeds crowded with myrtles, roses and oleanders create a frame for the ribbon of water dug into the marble and flanked on both sides with a row of jets that form a succession of crystalline arcades.

LA GRANJA *An imprint of the French style in this sumptuous garden created for Phillip V, where fountains are the main feature.*

To escape the torrid summer climate of Madrilene, the Spanish court was in the habit of moving to the sixteenth-century Palace of Valsain near Segovia. This custom was stopped by King Philip V, the first of the Bourbon dynasty in Spain and grandson of the Sun King, who was dissatisfied with the modest appearance of the palace – immersed in woods filled with the oaks and beeches that covered the mountains of Sierra Guardarrama – and who decided, in 1720, to have a completely new one built. He chose an area close by, where there was a hospice belonging to the Geronomite Brothers – an old chapel dedicated to San Ildefonso.

At first the works were entrusted to Theodore Ardemans, the designer of the royal palace in Madrid, but the sober tastes of the Spanish architect did not completely satisfy the desires of the king, who wanted a royal palace modelled on childhood memories of the sumptuous residence at Marly in France. On the advice of his wife, the strong-willed Queen Isabella Farnese, Philip V turned to the Italian Filippo Juvarra, who enlarged the palace and enhanced the main façade with an elegant play of colour, formed by combining the red granite of Segovia, used for a series of columns, and the white marble of Carrara, used for the cornices, statues and capitals.

The palace was inaugurated in 1723, while the development of the garden, despite the King's impatience and the use of 5,000 men, required a little more time. To level the rocky bank, garden workers had to use pickaxes and gunshot powder; it was also necessary to transport

ABOVE: *THE PALACE PARTERRE, POSITIONED IN FRONT OF THE PRINCIPAL FAÇADE OF THE PALACE WITH A VIEW OF THE NEW CASCADE.* RIGHT: *THE PARTERRE OF FAME. THE EIGHT WHITE URNS ARRANGED AMONG THE AUSTERE YEW TOPIARIES, ARE AMONG THE MOST BEAUTIFUL IN THE GARDEN; FOUR OF THESE CARRY THE EMBLEM OF PHILIP V AND ISABELLA FARNESE. A FOUNTAIN REPRESENTING FAME ASTRIDE PEGASUS SEPARATES THE PARTERRE FROM THE BOSKET OF THE SAME NAME.* OPPOSITE: *THE PALACE SEEN FROM THE PARTERRE OF FAME.*

earth for every tree, and to have hundreds of linden trees delivered from Holland and a large number of chestnut trees delivered from France. The disadvantages of the grounds were compensated, though, by the enormous quantity of water that would arrive – pure and crystalline – from the surrounding mountains. This almost unlimited availability permitted the realisation of an infinite number of water features and fountains, together with a multitude of statues, marble benches and lead vases created by a large group of artisans headed by René Frémin and Jean Thierry, two sculptors who had worked at Marly and at Versailles.

The architect commissioned for the garden was René Carlier, who, breaking the rules imposed by Le Nôtre – which would have meant a rigorously symmetrical space dominated by a single central perspective – plotted a series of axes perpendicular to the façades of the palace, each separated by boskets and avenues flanked by elms and

yews, along which he arranged water basins, canals, cascades and fountains alternating with geometric parterres. Thus he obtained an enormous but intimate garden, composed of three independent areas based on a schema that prefigured the imminent rococo style.

The most majestic view is that which, at a gentle slope, extends in front of the principal façade of the palace, right in front of the sovereign's apartments. Furnished with statues and white urns, it is enclosed at the top by the Fountain of the Three Graces. From here a veil of water descends, covering the red marble and jasper steps of the New Cascade, before collecting in the Amphitrite Fountain.

But the most spectacular parterre is undoubtedly the Carrera de Caballos, where along an axis parallel to that of the New Cascade, you find a series of impressive basins and water features: from the Neptune Fountain – where, at the centre of a large rectangular basin

ABOVE: *ANOTHER VIEW OF THE PARTERRE OF FAME.* LEFT: *THE NEW CASCADE. BUILT IN 1723 IT WAS CREATED WITH RED MARBLE AND JASPER STEPS, WHICH CARRY THE WATER BEFORE IT COLLECTS IN THE AMPHITRITE FOUNTAIN (FOREGROUND).* OPPOSITE, TOP LEFT: *THE BATHS OF DIANA, THE FOUNTAIN THAT REPRESENTS THE GODDESS IN THE CARE OF NYMPHS; OTHER NYMPHS PLAY AROUND WITH DOGS AND DOLPHINS (TOP, RIGHT);* BOTTOM RIGHT: *DETAIL OF THE LATONA FOUNTAIN, OR THE FOUNTAIN OF FROGS.* OPPOSITE, BOTTOM: *THE ENORMOUS ANDROMEDA FOUNTAIN.*

ABOVE: *A LEBANESE CEDAR IN ONE OF THE BOSKETS NEXT TO THE ANDROMEDA PARTERRE, DOMINATED BY A FOUNTAIN BY THE SAME NAME.* RIGHT: *THE RIA, A LONG COURSE OF WATER THAT DESCENDS FROM THE ANDROMEDA FOUNTAIN THROUGH A SERIES OF CASCADES AND THEN RUNS PARALLEL TO THE CARRERA DE CABALLOS, BEFORE FINALLY BRANCHING OFF AT RIGHT ANGLES TO RUN ALONG THE SELVA BOSKETS, NEXT TO THE PALACE.* OPPOSITE, TOP: *A VIEW OF THE PARK;* BOTTOM: *A WOODEN BRIDGE BUILT IN THE FIRST YEARS OF THE TWENTIETH CENTURY.*

WHERE: La Granja de San Ildefonso is about 11 kilometres from Segovia and about 80 kilometres from Madrid, at Plaza Espana 13.

GETTING THERE: By car from Segovia along the 601; from Madrid along highway A 6 to Villalba, where you take the 601.

VISITING HOURS: From the beginning of April to the end of September, every day except Monday, from 10:00 to 18:00. From the beginning of October to the end of March, from Tuesday to Saturday from 10:00 to 13.30 and from 15:00 to 17:00; Sundays and public holidays from 10:00 to 14:00.

INFORMATION: tel. 0034 921 470019; or visit www.jcyl.es/turismo.

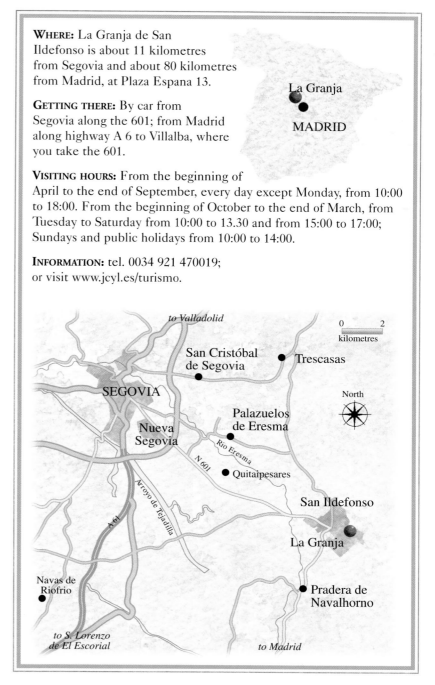

and among tritons, dolphins and powerful jets, the Greek god towers over a chariot drawn by seahorses – to the Andromeda Fountain – where the princess is saved from a terrible sea monster by Purseus, arranged at the highest point of the gardens to close the view.

On another side of the palace, Carlier arranged the Fountain of Fame, in which Fame, astride Pegasus, shoots a jet of water, at the time considered the highest in Europe, 47 metres into the sky. On clear days it is even visible from Segovia.

Many other water features, from the Latona Fountain to the Baths of Diana, were included in the vast park created next to the garden, populated by pines, oaks, yews and chestnuts and crossed by eight straight avenues that radiate outward from *Plaza de las Ocho Calles*, a wide octagonal space planned for hunting rallies.

FRONTEIRA PALACE *The luminous colours of the East, the formal rigours of the West: two styles, one garden.*

Eastern and western styles converge harmoniously in the garden created towards the middle of the seventeenth century by Joao Mascarenhas, first Marquis of Fronteira, on a woody hill near the gates of Lisbon. Immediately winning widespread approval, it was also praised by two famous guests, Marquis Corsini and the Grand Duke of Tuscany, Cosimo III de' Medici, both great gardening enthusiasts who visited it on 7 February 1669 and then described it with admiration in their travel diaries: the orderly series of terraces, the geometric boxwood parterres, the sinuous forms of the fountains, and the stone busts and statues from Renaissance Italian gardens, which blended in with the refined decorations of *azulejos*, the colourful ceramic tiles inherited from Islamic art.

Since then the design of the garden flanking the impressive castle painted in red has remained largely unchanged. The classic terrace design is identical to those which, from the middle of the fifteenth century, were adopted by the dei Medici villas and the sumptuous residences of powerful Roman cardinals, making the uneven ground workable. The low boxwood parterres form a complex weave of squares, circles and rhombi, where the number four – a symbol of the rivers of water, wine, milk and honey that flow in the Koranic paradise – is repeated again and again: dividing the parterre into quarters with two intersecting paths, and then again into four more parts.

To give a vertical dimension to the parterre, the spaces between the hedgerows were filled with little trees trimmed into cones, flowering

bushes, stone statues curiously arranged on oversized pedestals and five fountains. The largest, at the centre, commemorates the master of the house: a shield with the arms of Mascarenhas above an armillary sphere scored with rings representing the tropics and the equator. This was taken from a model that was common among sculptors of the period, used to extol the glorious Portuguese expeditions in search of new lands.

The severity of this flawless parterre, in line with the rigours of Renaissance traditions, is, however, unexpectedly contradicted by the wall that surrounds it on three sides – completely covered with glittering *azulejos* representing plants, constellations, signs of the zodiac and scenes of everyday life.

The *azulejos*, always present in Islamic garden paradises, are the main feature of the garden. Used liberally in every corner, they transform walls, benches and flowerboxes into glittering, imaginary places where familiar and obscure comedies, tragedies, love stories and war tales unfold: hunters capturing a flock of birds, an amanuensis absorbed in writing a letter for a masked lady, cats singing or visiting a barber's shop and monkeys playing in an orchestra. They depict mythological figures, famous men and women, and ladies and gentlemen engaged in amorous conversation.

Another unusual feature of the garden is the reservoir, which in Arabic gardening tradition ensured a water supply for the summer months. Instead of discretely disguising it in a corner, the Marquis de Fronteira positioned it boldly in the most visible point of the garden, separating it from the boxwood parterre with only a

RIGHT: *THE RESERVOIR THAT PROVIDES WATER FOR THE HOUSE AND GARDEN IS A BEAUTIFUL RECTANGULAR POOL WITH ENORMOUS STAIRWAYS ON EACH SIDE. ON THE BOTTOM WALL (DETAIL BELOW) THERE ARE 12 LIFE-SIZED KNIGHTS, PERHAPS FAMOUS MEMBERS OF THE MASCARENHAS FAMILY, TO WHOM THE PALACE BELONGED. ABOVE THE RESERVOIR IS THE TERRACE KNOWN AS THE GALLERY OF KINGS, IN WHICH THE BUSTS OF SEVERAL PORTUGUESE SOVEREIGNS ARE DISPLAYED (OPPOSITE).*

ABOVE: *A VAST ITALIAN-STYLE PARTERRE, WITH BOXWOOD HEDGES, STRETCHES OUT IN FRONT OF THE PALACE IN THE RENAISSANCE STYLE. IT IS 65 METRES LONG AND 57 METRES WIDE, WITH STATUES, TREES TRIMMED INTO SPHERES AND FOUNTAINS PROVIDING A COUNTERPOINT. LEFT: THE ENTRANCE OF CASA DO FRESCO OR CASA DE AGUA, A SORT OF GROTTO INSPIRED BY THE ITALIAN ROCAILLES, THE CEILING AND WALLS ARE ENCRUSTED WITH SHELLS AND FRAGMENTS OF GLASS, METAL AND PORCELAIN.*

AZULEJOS: *BETWEEN REALITY AND FANTASY*

For centuries, azulejos, *the glazed ceramic tiles inherited from Arabic culture, decorated Spanish and Portuguese gardens, covering walls, benches, flowerboxes and water basins with their fantastic images. Arriving in the Iberian peninsula with the Islamic conquerors, their use was initially limited to the strict geometric designs prescribed by the Koran. But soon the illustrations became more varied: human figures, mythological scenes, or scenes from daily life opened the door to an imaginary world.*

Until the end of the sixteenth century, the surfaces of these tiles had a raised grid to prevent different colours from mixing during firing. Later the tiles became perfectly smooth when tin glazes were used to fix the colours – limited to green, blue, yellow and violet because only copper, cobalt, antimony and manganese oxides are able to withstand the high temperatures of a kiln. From the seventeenth century, these multicoloured Azulejos *were joined by tiles with blue figures against a white background copied from Chinese porcelain and from recently imported Dutch delftware.*

Azulejos *owe their great fortune not only to the low cost of the raw materials necessary for their production (clay, tin and metal oxides) but also to Spanish and Portuguese customs at the time: in a country where women didn't participate much in society, and instead spent time walking in their gardens enclosed by high walls, these tiles permitted a harmless escape into a universe filled with extraordinary characters.*

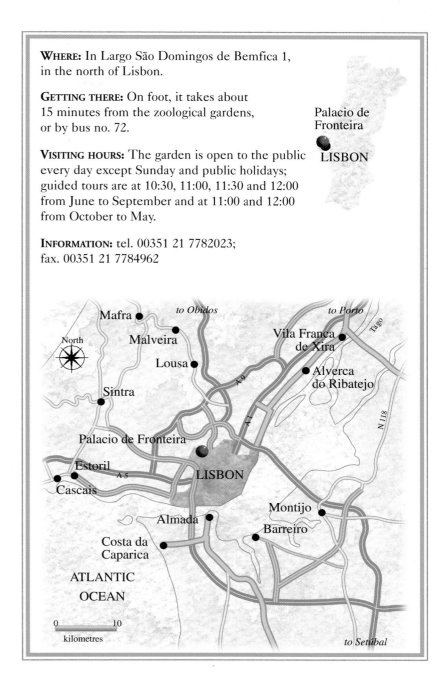

WHERE: In Largo São Domingos de Bemfica 1, in the north of Lisbon.

GETTING THERE: On foot, it takes about 15 minutes from the zoological gardens, or by bus no. 72.

VISITING HOURS: The garden is open to the public every day except Sunday and public holidays; guided tours are at 10:30, 11:00, 11:30 and 12:00 from June to September and at 11:00 and 12:00 from October to May.

INFORMATION: tel. 00351 21 7782023; fax. 00351 21 7784962

Palacio de Fronteira

LISBON

to Obidos

to Porto

Mafra

North

Malveira

Vila Franca de Xira

Lousa

Alverca do Ribatejo

Sintra

Palacio de Fronteira

Estoril

LISBON

Cascais

Montijo

Almada

Barreiro

Costa da Caparica

ATLANTIC OCEAN

0   10
kilometres

to Setúbal

see-through marble balustrade. This enormous rectangular pool, 50 metres long and 20 metres wide, refined with flower vases, enhanced by two enormous stairways and populated with four statues that seemed to walk on water, therefore added an extraordinary aesthetic value to its traditionally practical function. It is accentuated by the high wall that encloses it at the bottom, which is decorated with blind arcades and covered with white and blue *azulejos* representing life-sized knights astride their brave, rearing steeds, reminding one of the equestrian portraits of Velàzquez. It is also emphasized by the aristocratic elegance of the Gallery of Kings: a long terrace overlooking the water and created as a walkway between two pavilions. These are enclosed by a wall with blue tiles and niches, which frame the marble busts of several Portuguese sovereigns.

INDEX

Numbers in bold refer to the pages in which the gardens are described in depth; when gardens, places and historical figures are simply cited in the text the numbers are in light font, and when they are referred to in captions and boxes, the numbers are in italics.

INDEX OF HISTORICAL FIGURES